D1555443

Hope and Despair in Narrative and Family Therapy

Clients' experiences of hope and despair can be complex, reflecting individual and family histories, current patterns and dynamics, the stresses of everyday life and the social contexts of families' lives. This book analyses how therapists meet and engage with these dichotomous aspects of human experience.

The editors place the themes of hope and despair at the centre of a series of reflections on practice and theory. Contributors from all over the world are brought together, incorporating a range of perspectives from narrative, systemic and social constructionist frameworks. The book is divided into three sections, covering:

- Reflections on Hope and Despair
- Facing Adversity: Practices of Hope
- Reflections on Reconciliation and Forgiveness

Hope and Despair in Narrative and Family Therapy looks at the importance of hope in bringing about positive therapeutic change. This book will be of great use to family therapists, psychotherapists, counsellors and students on therapeutic training courses.

Carmel Flaskas is a social worker and family therapist and is Senior Lecturer at the University of NSW in Sydney where she convenes the Master of Couple and Family Therapy Programme.

Imelda McCarthy is Senior Lecturer and Director of the PhD programme in Families and Systemic Therapies at the School of Applied Social Science, University College, Dublin.

Jim Sheehan is Director of Family Therapy Training at the Mater Misericordiae University Hospital Dublin and Professor of Family Therapy and Systemic Practice at the Diakonhjemmet University College Oslo.

Contributors: Nollaig Byrne, Stephen Coulter, Carmel Flaskas, Trudy Govier, Arlene Healey, Paulette Moore Hines, Catherine Ingram, Kerrie James, Jenny, Elsa Jones, Just Anna, Imelda McCarthy, Monica McGoldrick, Stephen Madigan, Amaryll Perlesz, Isobel Reilly, Jim Sheehan, Suzanne Shuda, Karl Tomm, Allan Wade, Kaethe Weingarten.

Hope and Despair in Narrative and Family Therapy

Adversity, forgiveness and reconciliation

Edited by Carmel Flaskas,
Imelda McCarthy and
Jim Sheehan

LONDON AND NEW YORK

First published 2007
by Routledge
27 Church Road, Hove, East Sussex BN3 2FA

Simultaneously published in the USA and Canada
by Routledge
270 Madison Ave, New York, NY 10016

*Routledge is an imprint of the Taylor & Francis Group,
an informa business*

Typeset in Times by
RefineCatch Limited, Bungay, Suffolk
Printed and bound in Great Britain by
TJ International Ltd, Padstow, Cornwall

British Library Cataloguing in Publication Data
A catalogue record for this book is available from the British Library

Library of Congress Cataloging-in-Publication Data
Hope and despair in narrative and family therapy : adversity,
   forgiveness, and reconciliation / edited by Carmel Flaskas, Imelda
   McCarthy, and Jim Sheehan.
      p. ; cm.
   Includes bibliographical references and index.
   ISBN13: 978–1–58391–769–5 (hbk)
   ISBN10: 1–58391–769–1 (hbk)
   1. Family psychotherapy.   2. Narrative therapy.   3. Hope.
4. Despair.   I. Flaskas, Carmel.   II. McCarthy, Imelda.
III. Sheehan, Jim.
   [DNLM: 1. Family Therapy.   2. Attitude.   3. Emotions.
4. Narration. WM 430.5.F2 H791 2007]
   RC488.5.H61 2007
   616.89'156—dc22
2006026694

ISBN: 978–1–58391–769–5

Contents

The editors

Carmel Flaskas, a social worker and family therapist, is Senior Lecturer at the University of NSW in Sydney, where she convenes the Master of Couple and Family Therapy Programme. Carmel's contributions to family therapy include her work on the therapeutic relationship, on the translation of psychoanalytic ideas in the systemic context, and on knowledge and the potentials and limits of postmodernist ideas in therapy. She was recently awarded an honorary doctorate by the Tavistock Clinic in conjunction with the University of East London in recognition of her contribution to systemic psychotherapy.

Dr Imelda McCarthy is a Senior Lecturer and Director, PhD programme in Families and Systemic Therapies, School of Applied Social Science, University College, Dublin. With her colleagues, Nollaig Byrne and Philip Kearney, she developed the Fifth Province Approach which is widely published and translated into eight languages. With Sri Vasudeva she is now developing 'co-creative counselling and therapy' based on the Fifth Province Approach and new ideas from physics and spirituality, at the Blue Star Centre Trinidad, West Indies.

Professor Jim Sheehan is Director of Family Therapy Training at the Mater Misericordiae University Hospital Dublin where he is Course Director for a Masters programme in Family Therapy. He is also Professor of Family Therapy and Systemic Practice at the Diakonhjemmet University College Oslo where he contributes to a Masters education and training in the same area. His practice includes work with couples and families in conflict, the families of prisoners and those in court-mandated therapy. His publications have focused on narrative therapy, the contribution of philosophy to therapeutic practice and the learning experience of family therapists in training.

The contributors

Dr Nollaig Byrne is a child and adolescent psychiatrist and a systemic family therapist. Currently she holds the post of Clinical Director at the Mater Child and Adolescent Mental Health Service, Dublin. She has published internationally on the Fifth Province Approach.

Stephen Coulter is Clinical Coordinator of the Family Trauma Centre in Belfast and a family therapist within the service. He contributes to family therapy training courses and is a clinical supervisor for trainees on the MSc in Systemic Psychotherapy.

Dr Trudy Govier is a Canadian philosopher and author of many books and articles, including *Forgiveness and Revenge* (Routledge 2002) and *Dilemmas of Trust* (McGill Queen's 1998). She is currently a member of the Department of Philosophy at the University of Lethbridge.

Arlene Healey is the Manager of the Family Trauma Centre in Belfast and a family therapist. She is primarily responsible for establishing the service and leads a team of experienced psychotherapists. She contributes to family therapy training courses and is a clinical supervisor for trainees on the MSc in Systemic Psychotherapy.

Dr Paulette Moore Hines is a family therapist, clinical/community psychologist and Clinical Assistant Professor in the Department of Psychiatry, Robert Wood Johnson Medical School. She is the Executive Director of the Center for Healthy Schools, Families and Communities at the University of Medicine and Dentistry of New Jersey, and a member of the founding faculty of the Multicultural Family Institute of New Jersey.

Catherine Ingram teaches and supervises students of family therapy and consults with families at the Bouverie Centre in Melbourne. Her special interest is the gathering of stories by family members for The Wisdom Archive, which she co-ordinates. She is particularly drawn to narrative and spiritual ways of working.

Kerrie James lectures in counselling, group work, trauma and family therapy at the School of Social Work, University of NSW, Sydney. Her research interests are gender and attachment, intimate partner violence, couple therapy frameworks, apology and forgiveness in families. In 1999 she received the Special Award for Distinguished Contribution to Family Therapy in Australia.

'Jenny' has made the journey from being a nobody, to a confident, well-balanced individual who has found meaning and purpose. She now offers her wisdom to whomever she might meet on her journey through life.

Elsa Jones is a systemic psychotherapist and chartered psychologist working independently in Wales, UK, as a consultant, trainer and therapist. She teaches regularly through Britain and has written numerous papers and several books, including *Working with Adult Survivors of Child Sexual Abuse* (Karnac 1991).

Just Anna spent a large part of her life in indescribable pain, yearning for love to be unlocked. Anna now has a story to tell, a place to tell it from and a future to address it to.

Dr Monica McGoldrick is the Director of the Multicultural Family Institute in Highland Park, New Jersey, and is on the Psychiatry Faculty of the Robert Wood Johnson Medical School. She has written and edited many influential books in family therapy addressing, among other topics, understanding family relationships, family life cycle, genograms, ethnicity and race, culture and gender.

Dr Stephen Madigan founded North America's first narrative therapy clinic and training programme in 1992 at Yaletown Family Therapy, Vancouver (www.yaletownfamilytherapy.com). He presents workshops worldwide and sponsors the international and very cool Therapeutic Conversations conference each year (www.therapeuticconversations.com). He is also co-founder of the APA approved website www.planet-therapy.com that provides narrative and social justice CEs online. Stephen is the proud father of magnificent 10-year-old twin daughters, Hannah and Tessa Madigan.

Dr Amaryll Perlesz is Associate Professor in Family Therapy at The Bouverie Centre, La Trobe University, Melbourne. Her current research interests include engaging rural schools around issues of homophobia, lesbian families and using theatre of the oppressed techniques in the training and supervision of family therapists.

Isobel Reilly is Course Director of the Family Therapy Training Programmes in the School of Sociology, Social Policy and Social Work, Queens University Belfast. Her clinical practice is as a part-time family therapist in the Family Trauma Centre, Belfast.

Suzanne Shuda trained as a clinical psychologist, lives and works in South Africa and speaks to small and big people about what they would like in their lives. Finding what has grown out of conversations brings a sense of wonder to her work. She enjoys nature and loves to cycle.

Dr Karl Tomm is a Canadian psychiatrist at the University of Calgary where he founded the Family Therapy Program. He is well known in the field of family therapy for his work in clarifying and elaborating new developments in systems theory and systemic practice.

Dr Allan Wade is a therapist and researcher and lives on Vancouver Island, Canada. He developed his 'response-based' approach based on his work with victims and perpetrators of violence. In this he integrates brief, systemic, feminist ideas, recent research on violence/resistance and the connection between violence and language. With Linda Coates and Nick Todd he has published widely. His work is always received well in his international presentations.

Dr Kaethe Weingarten is an Associate Clinical Professor of Psychology at Harvard Medical School, director of the Witnessing Project and director of the Program in Families, Trauma and Resilience at the Family Institute of Cambridge. She is the author of numerous articles and chapters and her sixth book, *Common Shock* (Dutton 2004), won the 2004 Nautilus Award for Social Change.

Foreword

Lynn Hoffman

It is an honour to write the foreword to this anthology, since so many of the contributors are admired friends and colleagues, but there are also some lively newcomers I am privileged to meet. It is a book of needed voices, too, both original and erudite. What is unusual is the dichotomous theme, *Hope and Despair*, placed as the couplet from which to contemplate the issues relational therapists so frequently face. Some essayists, like Kaethe Weingarten, critique the individualistic idea of hope, saying that this is not a trait inside people but something we 'do' together. Her own story of hurtling in and out of cancer treatments is a courageous one, but her 'solution' is even more so. She describes how, in her last bout, she decided to dedicate each radiation treatment to friends and colleagues who were fighting AIDS and poverty in Africa. If this isn't 'doing hope', I don't know what is.

What I like about Part 1 is the fact that these authors so intelligently reflect on concepts that have often been seen as out of bounds in writing about therapy because of their frank moral nature. Carmel Flaskas starts with a philosophical puzzle: 'the necessary coexistence of hope and hopelessness'. She also brings up the highly charged picture of the Holocaust, suggesting that in the midst of that icon of horror, hope nevertheless was expressed in people's actions. She joins Weingarten in saying that you 'do' hope even when you can't feel it – sometimes, even, it is 'not your job' to do it, but that of the people who love you.

Following on, Nollaig Byrne and Imelda McCarthy use their 'Fifth Province' analogy from the Celtic tradition to offer a description of the hope/despair axis since, like Flaskas, they see these two sides as existing in dramatic tension with each other. Reading a transcript they included from one of their cases, I was enchanted by their spare use of 'questioning at the extremes'. They offer this idea as a way to bear down on the end of each polarity they encounter (life/death, healing/destruction), which then creates a movement from family members back toward a new balance.

The next group of essays, in Part 2, is oriented toward changing oppressive cultural discourses. This is a side-benefit, in my view, of the Foucauldian influence of poststructuralism on our field, mainly through the success of critical feminism, multiculturalism and narrative therapy. Descendants of these ideas fan out into a display of practices that light up dark places. For instance, Monica McGoldrick and Paulette Moore Hines tell stories about people who are challenged by bad events, but find ingenious ways to counter them, even when the outcomes can't be taken back or changed. In giving these events an intergenerational scope, they make it possible to see them as karmic solutions. Allan Wade, in turn, offers an important new idea. In dealing with victimization and abuse, he suggests therapists use 'response-based' questions instead of 'effects-based' ones. He asks about the person's reactions to being terrorized, then turns them so that strategies of resistance, instead of capitulation, appear. This simple change of template amazes people and in itself provides a jolt of hope.

The following chapters describe variations on the use of letter-writing in the presence of witnesses. Stephen Madigan, one of the early contributors to narrative therapy, describes what he calls 'counter-viewing', as opposed to 'interviewing'. This means taking a critical position in helping clients to identify the 'naming' and 'writing' structures that are used to label them as sick. Catherine Ingram and Amaryll Perlesz, together with a client, 'Jenny', take a similar path in their Wisdoms Project, where clients are helped to write their own counter-stories and store them in a special 'Archive'. Suzanne Shuda, and another client, 'Just Anna', show us other formats in which the negative identities promoted by the professional culture can be challenged in the presence of witnesses.

Dramatically representing the crossover between family and community, Stephen Coulter, Arlene Healey and Isobel Reilly describe their work in the Belfast Family Trauma Centre, founded in 1999 with a grant from Tony Blair. Their attempts to heal families are often negated by strife in the context of the faltering peace process. Attempts toward forgiveness and reconciliation are derailed by demands for justice or revenge. These themes are expanded by Elsa Jones in Chapter 12 in a discussion of the dilemma posed by people who are asked to forgive before the injustice has been addressed. Kerrie James speaks up to say that, in such cases, atonement practices must take priority.

Karl Tomm and Trudy Govier then contemplate the place of 'acknow-ledgement' as a key element in forgiveness and offer a variety of categories into which acknowledgement can fall. Finally, Jim Sheehan then moves to a more philosophical level in bringing up the dilemma of 'forgiving the unforgivable'. He finds an answer in Ricoeur's triadic structure whose three points include memory, forgetting and forgiving. Hope can be evoked, even in dire situations, in fantasizing about 'unfinished projects of the past'.

This collection, seemingly so diverse, is held together by a Janus formula-tion which on one level seems a contradiction, but on another fulfils and completes itself. It is an example of what the cognitive biologist Francisco Varela (1976) once called 'Star Logic'. On one side of the axis of hope you have the 'it'; on the other, the processes (which include hopelessness) leading to 'it'. Each level presumes the other: it is the ancient medieval circle with the dragon's tail in its mouth. This is the power of the hope/despair dichotomy, and why it is such a canny title under which to place a book.

Reference

Varela, F. (1976) Not one, not two, *CoEvolution Quarterly*, 12(1): 62–7.

Acknowledgements

Chapter 5, page 63

Quote from 'The Road to Wigan Pier' by George Orwell (copyright © George Orwell, 1937) by permission of Bill Hamilton as the Literary Executor of the Estate of the Late Sonia Brownell Orwell and Secker & Warburg Ltd.

Chapter 12, page 150

Two lines of 'Little Gidding' (1942) by T. S. Eliot from Collected Poems 1909–1962 by T. S. Eliot. Copyright © Faber and Faber Ltd, London. Used with permission.

Introduction: the territory of hope and despair

Carmel Flaskas, Imelda McCarthy and Jim Sheehan

This book and its project

This book is about hope and despair and the way in which as family therapists we meet and engage with this territory of human experience. For many families, the experience of hope and despair is complex. It can reflect a constellation of individual and family histories, current patterns and dynamics, the stresses of everyday life, the severity and chronicity of the family's struggle, and their exposure to abuse, adversity, tragedy and social injustice. Beyond these immediate and personal constellations lie the overarching cultural and social contexts that create the social conditions of individuals' and families' relationships to hope and despair.

Not surprisingly, engagement with clients' experiences has a parallel in therapists' own experience of hope and hopelessness. Psychotherapy itself stands as an activity of hope, for the collaborative project of client/s and therapist is always about the possibility of change. However, at the same time, as therapists we often find ourselves challenged by hopelessness and struggling with hope. We will also note that despite the frame of hope that psychotherapy offers, therapeutic practices also have the capacity to contribute to clients' experience of hopelessness and, in some situations, clients' despair is unmediated within the limits of what we have to offer.

While therapeutic practice on its own powerfully raises the significance of the experience of hope and despair, the empirical research programme on generic factors associated with successful therapeutic outcome also flags the importance of this topic. This research programme now spans 30 years, and has been brought together very well in a collection edited by Hubble *et al.* (1999a). They note that four major groups of factors have been identified as significant in positive therapy outcomes – the strengths and resources clients bring with them to the therapy; clients' capacity to hope for positive change (poorly represented in some psychotherapy research by the term 'the placebo effect'); the therapeutic alliance; and specific therapeutic techniques and models (Hubble *et al.* 1999b). In the ranking of these 'big four' groups of factors, clients' strengths and resources, and the therapeutic alliance, seem to account for roughly 40 per cent and 30 per cent respectively of the outcome variance. Clients' capacity for hopefulness then weighs in at 15 per cent of the outcome variance. That this is of equal weighting to the influence of the specific techniques and models used in the therapy is a staggering comparison.

That there is remarkably little literature explicitly addressing hope is, at least on the surface of things, quite peculiar. Indeed, we could think of only two articles – one by Amaryll Perlesz (1999), the other by Kaethe Weingarten (2000), both contributors to this volume – that tackle this topic head-on. We could also think of a chapter by Paulette Moore Hines (1998), also a contributor to this book, and a collection on narrative practice (Monk *et al.* 1997), which each explicitly name hope as a central concern. On the face of it, then, these writings could be seen to comprise the sum total of the literature in family therapy.

Yet, despite this, we would suggest that the themes of hope and despair are nonetheless deeply embedded in our discussions in far more extensive though non-explicit ways, and our sense here is that this is precisely because of the centrality of the experience of hope and hopelessness in everyday practice. For example, though the words 'hope' and 'despair' appear only rarely in practice discussions of working with serious adversity and abuse, one cannot help but constantly 'hear' these themes throughout this literature. The move to strengths-based approaches which directly call on clients' resilience, and the contemporary influences of narrative, solution-focused and the social constructionist readings of Milan-systemic therapy, all in different ways speak to our attempts to place hope more at the centre of our practice. And it is impossible to read or think about issues of acknowledgement, forgiveness and reconciliation, whether at the intimate level of personal abuse and hurt, or at the broader social level of decades (or even centuries) of abuse and oppression, without hearing powerful resonances of the human experiences of hope and despair.

The project of our book, then, is to place hope and despair at the centre of a series of reflections on practice and theory, and to begin to make more explicit the links between our concerns as family therapists and this territory of experience. As editors, we came together, the distance from Dublin to Sydney notwithstanding, to set about this project. We had in mind a collection that included contributors from a number of countries, not bound by any single context of practice, and representing the richness and diversity of current family therapy thinking and practice across the broad narrative and systemic range. We wanted to make room for some chapters that were more oriented to understandings about hope and despair, and some chapters that were closely tied to practices that potentially generate hope in contexts of hopelessness. We particularly wanted a series of chapters on the area of reconciliation and forgiveness, not with a view to presenting any singular position on the place and processes of reconciliation and forgiveness, but on the contrary with a view to opening the complexities of these processes and their relationship to hope. We also wanted to be open to contributors' own passions in their current work, and so offered a broad invitation in the first stage of the work.

The book we have ended up with includes contributors from Ireland, Australia, the United Kingdom, Canada, the United States and South Africa. We are very pleased that, in two chapters, clients and therapists have collaborated in exploring the journey of therapy. Some chapters show an underlying commitment to systemic ideas, others to narrative therapy, with many nuances in between, and all the discussions range well beyond the limits of any particular framework of practice. Not surprisingly, the experiences of abuse and serious adversity are central themes of many of the chapters, and it is fair to say that all the chapters circle this territory in one way or the other in their discussions. Across all the chapters, one also sees a tenacious orientation to resilience and a trust in the possibilities of moving beyond abuse and adversity.

The chapters are shaped into three parts. Part 1 contains three chapters that are primarily oriented to ways of thinking about hope and despair, weaving reflections on ideas about hope and despair with practice and personal experience. Part 2 contains six chapters which set the balance in the reverse way: here, navigating the territory of hope and despair in therapeutic practice takes centre-stage, and there is a wealth of ideas about practices of hope. Part 3 gives the final set of four chapters which between them map the processes of acknowledgement and the conditions for reconciliation, forgiveness and justice in situations of hurt and abuse. We will use this introduction now to give a more detailed preview for readers of the chapters and their themes.

The chapters

As noted above, the first part of the collection offers some general reflections on the themes of hope and despair in addition to some specific insights into how the dynamic of hope and despair reveals itself in therapeutic practice with families. All three chapters in the section are joined by a shared insistence that hope and despair must continuously be thought about together. Each contribution suggests ways in which hope and despair may be related to one another in the concreteness of human existence.

Chapter 1 sees Kaethe Weingarten develop a contrast between an individualistic psychology of hope and an understanding of hope as something we do together and she draws on a range of ideas as well as a depth of personal experience. She argues that the uneven distribution of hope and despair in our lives, as well as in global terms, means that we all have different but related tasks within the response to this context: those gripped by hopelessness must resist isolation; those in whom hope has more security must refuse indifference. In support of the view of hope as something we practise together, Kaethe also notes how neurological evidence grounds a view of the brain as wired to be responsive to interpersonal collaboration. At the level of practice, the challenge is to make visible the different tasks that hope and hopelessness perform in lives and relationships.

In Chapter 2, Carmel Flaskas invites the reader deeper into the meaning of the perpetual coexistence of hope and hopelessness. She cautions against the temptation to view the relationship between these two as an event in which an increase in the experience of one means a reduction in the experience of the other. In the place of such dichotomous thinking, she suggests that hope and hopelessness present themselves to each of us as a complex and layered experience of emotion, meaning and behaviour. The family therapist needs to pay attention not simply to the way this interplay between hope and despair is divided up between family members at any point in time, but also to the manner in which this internal balance of hope and despair is either supported or undermined by the community and broader political processes in which the family is embedded. A critical factor in the evolution of each therapeutic encounter is the resonance between the balance of hope and despair in the life of the therapist and the balance in the family's experience.

The reflection by Nollaig Byrne and Imelda McCarthy in Chapter 3 concludes this first part of the book by adding a further twist to the descriptions addressing the relationship between hope and despair. Emphasizing the discursive character of the phenomena we name hope and despair, they provide a rich account of the way in which a broad discourse on the pair has been shaped over time within western secular and religious traditions. This is the background against which they allow their practice material to illustrate how a trust in the dialectical structure of the hope/despair relationship carries the potential to generate both new conversations and accompanying relational forms. The family therapist is invited to shed any view of hope and despair as 'oppositions to be overcome', a hierarchy to be reversed or an unfolding synthesis. Instead, what the structure of hope and despair seeks from us at the heart of our therapeutic practice is reconciliation with each other rather than evaluation.

Part 2 moves away from the realm of ideas about the relationship of hope and despair toward a focus on practices. All the contributions in this section describe different ways in which the therapist/family relationship aims at generating hope in contexts where people have experienced trauma, suffering and adversity.

Like many others in the collection, the chapter by Monica McGoldrick and Paulette Moore Hines (Chapter 4) disconnects hope as a concept from all versions of naive optimism and suggests that the clinical job of the family therapist is one of fostering hope in others by connecting them to their own spiritual resources as 'wellsprings of hope'. The successful accomplishment of this connecting task in contexts of extreme adversity is highly dependent upon therapists' capacity to understand and appreciate both their own and their clients' positions in the wider context of power and privilege. When faced with the immediacy of trauma effects in the clinical encounter, they suggest that it is often only in the assumption of a more expanded temporal lens – in which clients see their experience and responses as part of what has come before them and what will come after them – that a sense of hopefulness arises. The dilemmas of white therapists working with clients of colour in the context of racism raises the ethical imperative of acknowledging experiences of oppression. Such acknowledging often opens the door for hope to emerge 'on the far side of despair'.

Although focusing largely on victims of domestic violence, Allan Wade's central argument in Chapter 5 is clearly relevant for other client groups. He gradually unfolds a position on response-based therapy, beginning with an argument that the coding by therapists of the responses of victims only in a language of 'effects' reduces the significance of these responses to a drama of individual pain. By contrast, using a language of 'responses' allows client actions and experiences to be perceived as resistances of different kinds in which a rich array of political and other meanings can be seen to lie. The language of effects often engenders a hopelessness, at the same time as it sometimes implicates the victims in the crimes committed against them. A response-based approach, on the other hand, fosters hope through a rendering of the victim as an agent who defends and promotes critical human values in a way that transcends her or his own individual suffering.

The view of therapeutic practice as in some way limited to verbal exchanges has suffered a slow erosion in the last decade. Three of the chapters in this second part of the collection add momentum to this process by describing ways in which reading and writing are conceived as central to certain clinical work. The accounts of Catherine Ingram, Jenny and Amaryll Perlesz (Chapter 6), Suzanne Shuda and Just Anna (Chapter 7) and Stephen Madigan (Chapter 8) all reveal interesting patterns in which reading and writing processes are grafted into broader therapeutic dialogues aimed at fostering hope in a context of adversity.

Catherine Ingram, Jenny and Amaryll Perlesz describe the Wisdoms Project at the Bouverie Centre in Melbourne in which an archive of clients' writings articulating their experience and learning in the context of adversity is made available to others in an ongoing manner. The written story of the client in therapy creates a break between the author-as-writer and the author-as-listener. This gap sets up a dialogical space in which stuck, repetitive monologues (usually filled with negative self-perception) can evolve into dialogues that invite changes in the perception and behaviour of self and others. These externalized narratives (as clients hear their narratives being read aloud by others) have the capacity to evoke a more compassionate witnessing, not just on the part of the therapist, but for the client as she or he hears their own story in a different way. The voices of Jenny and Catherine Ingram are heard very powerfully as they describe the journey Jenny made with respect to her own experience of adversity and abuse in her therapeutic work with Catherine. This chapter gives further testimony to Kaethe Weingarten's premise from the opening contribution: isolation is the stuff of hopelessness; hope is a practice we do together.

Also authored jointly by therapist and client, the chapter by Suzanne Shuda and Just Anna provides a unique contribution to the volume. Central to their description of the therapeutic process is a joint struggle to overcome the circumscribing of the client's identity through the formalities of diagnosis and clinical records in an adult mental health context. Writing and reading appeared in this therapy in a variety of ways: Just Anna kept a diary which allowed her to hold on to a sense of her existence in vulnerable times; a member of a reflecting team sent a written account to Just Anna of her impressions of her in a session; and the power of the 'unseen' hospital record was undermined by the therapeutic pair gaining access to it and providing their own reading of it.

Echoing to some degree the spirit of the earlier chapter by Allan Wade, Stephen Madigan alerts us to the way the everyday writing and naming practices of professionals and therapists in their institutional settings invite clients into a limited perspective on what they should anticipate for their own lives. Such practices, Stephen Madigan asserts, create a powerful context that subtly urges clients to accept a level of despair in their lives and cancels out hope in the possibility of positive change. The author's own approach to narrative therapy responds to this context with a practice of 'counter-viewing'. This engages the client in a *critical* reading of all the professional meaning systems that have circumscribed the client's identity and possibilities, at the same time as *respecting* the place in which clients stand in the moment of therapeutic encounter. Building upon the therapeutic letter-writing tradition of Michael White and David Epston (1990), Stephen Madigan develops this practice into a sustained 'campaign' aimed at creating a community of concern with the potential to break the connection to despairing views of the person suffering and allow for the anticipation of hope to emerge.

Civil and community conflict in Northern Ireland is the context for the account by Stephen Coulter, Arlene Healey and Isobel Reilly (Chapter 9) of their therapeutic work with victims in a family trauma centre. Other contributions to this collection reference the political context of therapeutic work, mostly in the form of broader social discourses that oppress certain client groups. However, this chapter is unique in that it elegantly and poignantly portrays the concrete challenges to the therapy of traumatized victims arising from the ongoing interplay between the back-and-forth movement in the broader political efforts to achieve peace between the two sides of a divided community, and the journey towards recovery of individual clients and their families. A number of case vignettes vividly portray how these practitioners respond to the oscillating waves of hope and despair that strike their clients, themselves and the community around them as the larger political peace process appears to undergo intermittent changes in direction.

Familial and other relational wounds provide the context for Part 3, the final section of this book, which offers reflections on the relevance of forgiveness and reconciliation for the balance of hope and despair in individual lives and relationships. Three contributions address specifically the dilemmas associated with forgiveness, while the fourth teases out some of the key ingredients in and consequences of reconciliation following relational trauma.

There is a danger that family therapists addressing the context of interpersonal wounds between intimates can focus too much on the forgiving process of the one who has been hurt and not sufficiently on the processes of taking responsibility and atonement in the one who has done wrong. Through a systematic review of the literature, Kerrie James (Chapter 10) argues strongly that this indeed has been the history of therapist involvement in the arena and that what is required is a deeper appreciation of the interactional process through which the taking of responsibility and the offering of forgiveness are joined. A variety of dangers associated with the promotion of forgiveness in victims are outlined and practitioners are urged to interrogate the models of forgiveness they use for the extent to which they place emphasis on the accountability of the wrongdoer.

From a different angle, Karl Tomm and Trudy Govier (Chapter 11) also address the consequences of interpersonal relational wounds. While family therapists have perhaps given more attention to the process of forgiveness than to the nature of reconciliation, the authors of this chapter take steps to redress this imbalance by pointing to 'acknowledgement' as a key element in the reconciliation process. They describe acknowledgement as a relational achievement that increases the possibilities for rebuilding and maintaining hope within damaged relationships that have grown vulnerable to despair. Careful distinctions are made between different kinds of acknowledgement and attention is drawn towards the different levels (intrapersonal, interpersonal, group, community) where it has a contribution to make towards both reconciliation and the well-being of individuals and relationships.

In Chapter 12, Elsa Jones very specifically examines what she suggests is a recurring dilemma for victims at the closing stage of a period of therapeutic healing. The person must decide how to position him/herself in relation to the one who has wounded them. Put simply, do they offer forgiveness, pursue justice or exact revenge? While acknowledging that such options can be filled with a complex mix of different cultural meanings, the author demonstrates the powerful role that fantasy and ritual can play at this concluding point in the therapy. She suggests that the belief that justice can be finally achieved often proves therapeutically limiting for certain victims, while an understanding of how a wound occurring between individuals was part of what was happening in the wider community may progress the possibilities of healing, forgiveness and reconciliation.

The cautionary emphasis by Kerrie James on an unreflected forgiveness finds further support from Jim Sheehan in the final chapter of this collection (Chapter 13). Here we find an argument that therapeutic effort must give equal weight to the unforgivable character of wounding experiences. Just as hope and despair were considered as a coexisting pair by the authors of the chapters in Part 1, it is suggested that forgiveness and the unforgivable must always be thought about together despite the 'slippery' and changing character of their relationship. The multifaceted nature of forgiveness comes to light for therapists through a drawing upon a number of different disciplinary discourses on the phenomenon. Philosophical (Derrida and Ricoeur), literary (Blake) and legal (Minow) discourses on forgiveness are all seen to make contributions to the understanding and practice of therapists where forgiving the unforgivable seems to be what is at stake. Of particular interest is the therapeutic deployment of Ricoeur's philosophical framework for forgiveness that sees it as a third point in a triadic structure that joins memory, forgetting and forgiving. Therapeutic work within this structure carries the potential for resurrecting the hope attaching to the unfinished projects of the past.

Concluding comment

In imagining this project, we, the editors, had wanted to explore very explicitly the territory of hope and despair as one of the primary pairs of human experience that propel people to seek help in their lives. Without some level of despair there would be no initiation; without hope there would be no ongoing engagement. Again and again across the collection as a whole, chapters highlight in many different ways the inseparability of hope and despair, adversity and resilience, forgiveness and the unforgivable. Neither side of these dualities can be taken alone as we move through the therapeutic journey as professionals and clients. In many ways, juxtaposing these dualities points us to a holistic order, of a Batesonian *both/and* worldview. And as with any going-beyond of dualistic frames, there is a spiritual sense of an underlying unity expressing itself in diverse and often undreamed-of forms.

If you the reader can be inspired in the reading of these offerings, then the project we set ourselves has been well realized.

References

Hines, P.M. (1998) Climbing the rough side of the mountain, in M. McGoldrick (ed.) *Re-visioning Family Therapy: Race, Culture and Gender in Clinical Practice*. New York: Guilford.

Hubble, M.A., Duncan, B.L. and Miller, S.D. (eds) (1999a) *The Heart and Soul of Change: What Works in Therapy*. Washington: American Psychological Association.

Hubble, M.A., Duncan, B.L. and Miller, S.D. (1999b) Introduction, in M.A. Hubble, B.L. Duncan and S.D. Miller (eds) *The Heart and Soul of Change: What Works in Therapy*. Washington: American Psychological Association.

Monk G., Winslade J., Crockett, K. and Epston, D. (eds) (1997) *Narrative Therapy in Practice: The Archaeology of Hope*. San Francisco: Jossey-Bass.

Perlesz, A. (1999) Complex responses to trauma: challenges in bearing witness, *Australian and New Zealand Journal of Family Therapy*, 20(1): 11–19.

Weingarten, K. (2000) Witnessing, wonder and hope, *Family Process*, 39(4): 389–402.

White, M. and Epston, D. (1990) *Narrative Means to Therapeutic Ends*. New York: W.W. Norton.

Part 1

Reflections on hope and despair

Chapter 1

Hope in a time of global despair

Kaethe Weingarten

The straggly crab-apple tree on my neighbor's path is blooming. Tasteless, extravagantly expensive blueberries have replaced the small wooden crates of clementines on the front counter of my local grocery store. It's April. A survivor of three cancers, I have entered the arc of the year in which I hope I will live to eat clementines again.

Hope can be a wish, an expectation of something desired. I hope I live the six months until clementines reappear in the stores. This hope floats in the realm of feeling; I do nothing but note it.

Hope can also be a practice: it is achieved by taking action on behalf of one's desires or commitments. Last winter, unbeknownst to me, my partner froze a batch of clementines and we ate them like popsicles in July. 'You have lived to eat clementines again,' he said as we savored the cold, sweet, orange sections and the moment.

This chapter concerns hope as a practice. It is about *doing hope* with others (Weingarten 2000, 2003). This conceptualization arises out of my own need for a way of thinking about hope that can sustain both my supporters and me. Tested more than we would wish, I have generated ideas about hope that offer an alternative to those I have found in mainstream popular and academic sources.

Western ideas about hope originate with the foundational myth of Pandora, a beautiful young woman who was given as a gift to Epimetheus by Zeus. Two versions of the myth exist: one in which Pandora's adolescent curiosity leads her to open a jar filled with human miseries that she has been specifically instructed to leave alone and, horrified, she is only able to reseal the jar in time to keep hope inside; and another in which she opens a box and inadvertently lets out all the blessings known to humankind except hope. In both versions, two ideas are central. The first is that Zeus wants hope to be the responsibility of humans and second that hope exists inside one solitary object.

This latter idea corresponds with the common view that hope is a feeling, an achievement of one person alone. The same premise undergirds the principal empirical investigations of hope. For the last two decades, C. R. Snyder and his colleagues in the psychology department at the University of Kansas have studied the psychology of hope. Here is one item from their Adult Trait Hope Scale (Snyder *et al.* 1997): I meet the goals that I set for myself. The scale perfectly captures the individualistic view of hope. Each hope item is designed to measure people's convictions that they can accomplish goals on their own. Now imagine an Adult Trait Hope Scale that is predicated on the notion that hope is something you do with others. Here is the same item revised to reflect that hope is the responsibility of the community: I can count on the support of others to help me meet my goals.

The view of hope expressed in the second version pivots the responsibility for its accomplishment away from the individual alone, who may or may not 'feel' hope, to the individual in community. It reflects both a pragmatic and a philosophical point of view. Individuals are notoriously prone to despair. Pragmatically, expecting people to summon hope on their own when they feel most dispirited seems unwise, even cruel. What's more, it may instantiate a fundamental misconception about the nature of human relatedness: we are not isolated, but rather intrinsically interdependent.

The Buddha expressed this as 'the one contains the all' (Hanh 1999: 221). Indra's net, hanging above the palace of the god Indra, provides a beautiful image of – and a metaphor for – human interrelatedness. The net is infinite in dimension and in the center of its every node rests a jewel, reflecting every other jewel in the net. This ancient wisdom finds contemporary expression in philosophy and science. For example, Alfred North Whitehead wrote in a lecture he delivered in 1926: 'The [people] are the primary units of the actual community . . . But each unit has in its nature a reference to every other member of the community, so that each other member of the community . . . is a microcosm representing in itself the entire all-inclusive universe' (Whitehead 1926).

Today, neuroscientists have identified mirror neurons that fire in our brains when we observe actions performed by others (Rizzolatti and Craighero 2004). This is a physical manifestation of interrelatedness; our very own nerve cells empathically resonate with others by mimicking them. Neuroanatomically, I am what you do.

Hope tasks

From Indra's net to neural nets we see expressions of human interconnectedness. What does this mean for hope? Simply put, we each have a role in its manifestation but our positions in relation to hope determine what we must do. Those who are hopeless and those who witness their despair have different tasks.

For some doing hope emerges out of the most intimate knowledge. I suffer severe and apparently intractable pain as a result of treatments for cancer. I move in and out of hopelessness. My husband's days and nights are filled with awareness of the ebb and flow of my pain. At night the shifting depth of his sleep reflects his ever-vigilant witness. By day, his constant wondering when he will get a call from me letting him know that my ability to sustain productive work has ended for the day is its measure. We both believe that hope is important and we know, achingly so, that what we must each do to accomplish it is not the same.

Hope, hopelessness and despair may touch our lives at far remove. The radio at dinnertime brings news of a flooded Chinese village, thousands dead, while we are setting the table for our meal. The morning paper contains a story about rape in Darfur as we are arguing with our partner about who will walk the dog. The gap between what we witness and what others suffer is staggering. Taking in what is happening in the world and registering the immensity of the gap may temporarily or chronically sap our reserves of hopefulness.

Hope and despair are unevenly distributed in our lives and on our planet. Some people, some groups of people, some nations, lack and need hope; others, hope intact or untested, are witnesses. For however long these circumstances obtain, they position us differently and call for different actions.

Hopeless, we must resist isolation. Witness to despair, we must refuse indifference. Neither is easy.

Peggy Penn, a psychotherapist and poet in New York, has worked for decades with people with chronic and severe illness, a group who are often hopeless (Penn 2001). She well knows the gravity of the pull toward isolation and the dangers of it. Before withdrawal, however, there is a struggle. The ill and unwell have an intense desire to share the details of the body's betrayals but this is coupled with an equally immense fear that to do so as often as the body does betray would drive away the very audience we most want to stay. Penn names this a paradox. I live it as a bind.

Whether hopelessness derives from chronic illness or any other condition against which struggle seems insurmountable, the task is to resist the temptation to withdraw from others. *The task is to resist isolation.*

The witnesses' task is a related one. In the face of calamities and tragedies that happen over and over again, in our homes and on our planet, we must reject indifference. Indifference exerts its own seductive pull, roping us in by our feeling, first, inadequate and then, overwhelmed. Recognizing these sticky strands is the first step of *refusing indifference.*

The tasks I am proposing are difficult. Mutually intertwined, they call for doing hope together, yet they don't concretize a way of doing so. Instead, they are an approach, an attitude. Coupled with concepts from Snyder's group, a practice does emerge.

The practice of hope

Snyder's group conceptualizes hope as a form of thinking that has three components, schematized as goal, waypower and willpower thinking. They write: 'Hope is a way of thinking in which a person has the perceived way-power and willpower to achieve goals' (Snyder *et al.* 1997: 7). I have already critiqued the individualistic orientation of their model, which is evident in this formulation. Willpower, or 'agency', the more technical term for it, implies that the motivation, determination and energy to achieve goals must be summoned from within, clearly a high hurdle for those who are truly hopeless and in desperate situations. Willpower conceptualized as a collective responsibility is attainable.

Waypower thinking, or, as the group also writes, pathways thinking, can also be reinterpreted as a collaborative enterprise. People who are discouraged can rarely summon the energy or creativity to see their goals clearly or imagine routes to them. Hopelessness itself often emerges in the context of blocked pathways to goals, which can engender confusion about the goals themselves. Despair is the conviction that nothing that one wants or wanted is within reach, whether love or security or clean water or health. Clarifying goals and identifying pathways toward them is part of the practice of doing hope; when we are hopeless others may have to help us do this.

But this is not necessarily simple. First, there is often a lot of trial and error to define goals and pathways that will succeed. Goals and pathways to them may have to replace each other at a rate one would never have expected or wanted. Second, life deals us circumstances in which we have to select goals and pathways we never thought we could accept. Yet, the practice of doing hope, of re-forming goals and cultivating pathways to them, stretches us, helping us sustain the very practice of doing hope.

My mother died decades ago. During her time of dying she was rarely hopeless, a gift that has continued to unfold in the lives of her children and grandchildren to this day. A writer, she wanted her experience with the medical care system to be of use to others. When she realized she had an incurable cancer, she was temporarily in despair. She turned to her oncologist, who suggested that she keep a journal – long before the days that people wrote illness memoirs. She did so until three months before her death (Weingarten 1978). Writing the journal provided a pathway toward a goal that was accessible to her, while there was no pathway toward the eminently preferred goal of staying alive.

I, who had wanted to grow old with my mother, at first wanted her to avail herself of any treatment that might extend her life. Ultimately, in the final hours of her life, I wished her dead. I saw that my hope for connection to my mother would forever be in my dreams and in my heart and never with the unconscious body lying inert in the hospital bed. In one excruciating 24-hour period my hope tumbled through four phases: please don't let her die became please don't let her suffer, which passed on to please let her die comfortably, which then morphed the most inconceivable hope into a conceivable one: let her die now. It was only after listening to Karl Tomm at a workshop 21 years later (Tomm 1997) that I fully acknowledged my thoughts and only in writing this chapter that I fully accepted them. Hope depends on pathways thinking to an achievable goal, whether that goal breaks our heart or not.

Hope as a practice of solving for pattern

This past summer I read a remarkable letter written by Jeffrey Sachs, Special Advisor to UN Secretary-General Kofi Annan on the Millennium Development Goals and Director of the Earth Institute at Columbia University. He wrote the letter after visiting rural villages in Kenya that he described as 'beset by hunger, AIDS, and malaria,' with conditions far 'grimmer' than any UN document conveys (Sachs 2004). He met with 200 villagers for three and a half hours to learn about their problems and to think with them about how their situation could improve.

The letter details terrible conditions that prevail in the community. Malaria is constant and AIDS prevalence is 30 percent or more. Virtually every household is taking care of a child orphaned by AIDS. Clean water is not always available. Few of the farmers can afford fertilizers for the soil, rainfall is inconsistent, and as a result food production is low. There is barely enough food to feed the villagers, much less to take to market.

Sachs observes that the villagers are clear on goals, but they lack access to the resources that would provide pathways to them. This is precisely what Sachs does have access to. In his letter, he frames his approach to the villagers' problems in a manner consistent with the themes I have been addressing in this chapter. First, he is not indifferent to the villagers' plight. Second, he operates from a premise of global interconnectedness. As an economist, he puts this in market terms: 'The remarkable point is that this village could be rescued . . . Survival depends on addressing a series of specific challenges . . . all of [which] can be met, with *known, proven, reliable, and appropriate* technologies and interventions . . . at a cost that is tiny for the world but too high for the villages themselves' (Sachs 2004: 5). How might a 'global village' operate on this observation? Sachs suggests that rich and poor nations must make visible the multiple arrangements they have with each other. For instance, while Kenya's foreign investment need in rural areas is about $1 billion per year, donor support to Kenya is around $100 million. 'Amazingly, Kenya's debt servicing to the rich world is around $600 million per year, much larger than the aid inflows! Kenya's budget is therefore still being drained by the international community, not bolstered by it' (Sachs 2004: 8).

Sachs' analysis connects the villagers' needs to the wider context of the international donors' debt servicing inflows. He recognizes that one solution to the rural villagers' problems lies in increasing donors' outflows and decreasing their inflows from desperately poor peoples. Reading Sachs' letter I was reminded of Wendell Berry's term 'solving for pattern,' his apt phrase for developing solutions that do not make the problem worse and that do make improvements in harmony with the overall context within which problems are embedded (Berry 2002). Sachs' genius is his ability to make connections between facts on the ground and those of the global market. He sees that pathways thinking is more constructive when linked to an understanding of the widest possible context within which problems are embedded and that solving for pattern is bound to be more effective if we look at the whole.

Questioning hope in therapy

As therapists, this is our challenge too. We try to understand the context of our clients' distress, communicate our empathy for their dilemmas and provide energy and direction for alternative ways of thinking about their situations. Good questions are a mainstay of our work. They produce fresh responses, which bring facets of the pattern into view that had been obscured. They contribute to conversations that are rich and enlivening.

Some questions, however, initiate conversations that entrench the very problems we are trying to solve. Hopelessness is notorious for inducing those who confront it – like therapists – to ask questions that worsen the problem. It is as if our facility with questioning shrinks in direct proportion to the depletion of zest we feel sitting with those who despair. Inadvertently, our questions lack the complexity to generate the material out of which solving for pattern can happen.

I had such an experience with Anna, a woman in her late thirties working at a creative job within a Byzantine organization. I had seen Anna for several months, during which time she was going through a painful breakup with her boyfriend. Her pain at his loss was compounded by anger at the injustice of the timing of his leaving her: within weeks of her father's death. We worked together until Anna felt more herself, readier to move on and look forward to whatever was next in her life.

About three years later, Anna came to see me again. She had just begun treatment for a curable cancer and was enraged at her misfortune. She said, 'Cancer has cut hope off at the knees. It's mangled my hope that my life will ever be different.' Remembering her abusive family history, eventually in the session I asked her to reflect on how this history might be contributing to her hopelessness at this time. Cooperatively, Anna began telling her family story using disappointment, loss, and shame as her organizing themes. She cried and we were both moved by what she shared. But I felt no traction. I could offer companionship in her sadness, anger and grief but the path we were on was not producing direction, and it was certainly not solving for pattern.

'How is this going for you?' I asked.

'Terrible.' She said, 'I don't want to talk about why I feel hopeless. I feel worse than when I came in.'

'*What is the work you need hope to do for you?*' I asked her. '*What do you want hope for?*'

These questions took her off guard and were immediately generative for Anna. Without hesitation she answered:

'When I have hope, I have the ability to imagine something good and then I can take steps to do it.'

'So what does hope actually do?'

'It illuminates the corridors. It helps me see the way out.'

'What about now? Is there a beam of light shining anywhere in the corridor? Can you see anything at all?'

'Truthfully, right now, there is a tiny beam and I can see a few steps ahead of me.'

'Who's holding the light?'

'I am.'

'Is that OK with you?'

'Damn it, you know it's not.'

We were off and running. The questions had elicited an image that invigorated Anna and gave her many angles to explore. It triggered her imagination and helped her believe she could solve for pattern, although we never spoke this phrase between us. It unblocked her thinking and unstuck the painful emotional rut she was in. It freed her to work on the very real dilemmas in her life. For instance, she wanted to know: Who could hold the flashlight when she got tired and why were there so few candidates for that position? How was she deciding which part of the corridor to illuminate and how did she know it was the best place? If she took the cancer as a wake-up call, where might she shine the light?

These conversations produced a corollary to the first two questions about hope. *What is your hopelessness insisting that you understand about your life?*

All three questions extend the concept of doing hope by concretizing that hope is literally something we do. In the same way that as a writer I ask myself what work I need a word to do in a sentence, people can interrogate hope, enquiring what they need it to do. Likewise, despair and hopelessness are urgently sending messages that can, must, be decoded. Once understood, pathways can be found toward goals.

As therapists we are keenly aware that hopelessness constricts our clients' thinking, making it difficult to move to a 'place' from which these three questions can be addressed. Life in certain regions can also contribute to cognitive constriction, making it difficult to address these questions from the perspective of a citizen applying them to the society in which he or she lives.

In cultures dominated by fear, anger and hate, hope is scarce and yet crucial. When societies are under threat, fear – an automatic, physiologic response – serves important functions. In societies where the threat is exaggerated or past, fear can nonetheless overwhelm hope and interfere with crucial activities, such as peacebuilding (Bar-Tal 2001).

Under conditions of perceived or actual threat, it may just be too difficult for individuals to resist fear alone. Collectively, though, groups of individuals can support each other to diminish, not amplify, their fear responses. *Encouraging and supporting others to resist the powerful pull of fear and hate is a third way that we can do hope together*. And it is important to do, since hope confers so many advantages, for individuals and societies. High hope individuals do better at problem solving, at managing challenging situations and even in coping with illness and disability (Snyder *et al.* 1999).

The neurobiology of hope

While this discussion has so far emphasized the interpersonal merits of doing hope together, it rests on a review of neurobiological evidence that suggests that the brain is actually wired to be responsive to interpersonal collaborations. A series of studies undertaken by Richard J. Davidson, a psychologist at the University of Wisconsin who has been studying the neural circuitry of emotion for decades, are especially relevant (Davidson 2003). In one set of studies, Davidson looked at how positive and negative emotions might interact with each other in the brain. It is known that the limbic system, and particularly the amygdala, plays a decisive role in the experience of fear. Chronic exposure to stress can induce rapid and sustained excitation of the limbic system, creating the sensation of hyper-arousal and fear. Davidson and his colleagues wanted to see whether other parts of the brain might dampen the limbic system's excitability, which indeed they did find. In the process they realized that it would be more accurate to think of the brain as a system of highly interconnected complex neural networks rather than separate structures with pinpoint functions.

Davidson and his team found that positive emotions that originate in the prefrontal cortex set off chemical cascades that flow to and infuse the limbic system. (Chemicals flow the other way also.) The prefrontal cortex is rich in dopamine, a chemical that is thought to have a role in the release of endorphins and encephalins, the brain's natural form of morphine (Groopman 2004). The amygdala is particularly sensitive to dopamine and it turns out that the amygdala is quieted by the chemicals released by the prefrontal cortex.

Importantly for our understanding of doing hope, Davidson believes that setting goals and pursuing paths toward them activates the reward circuitry of the prefrontal cortex, setting in motion the complex chemical interplay between the prefrontal cortex and the amgydala (Groopman 2004). In a very tangible way then, assisting people with the formulation of goals and pathways toward them – doing hope – activates a neurochemical cascade that dampens fear and makes people feel more hopeful.

People vary widely in their ability to sustain hope in difficult circumstances and are inequitably challenged by socioeconomic, political and interpersonal circumstances. These are reasons why I prefer to think about hope as something we do together. There are biological justifications for this preference as well. Scientists are now learning that there is a neural basis for the observation that people vary in their ability to withstand stress. Charney, in a comprehensive review of the psychobiology of vulnerability and resilience, posits that resilient people may have 'a reward system that is either hypersensitive to reward or is resistant to change, despite chronic exposure to neglect and abuse' (Charney 2004: 205). Further, in resilient individuals, the neural networks associated with social cooperation and mutual altruism may be more densely linked to reward centers in the brain than for more vulnerable individuals, making bonding and attachment to others more gratifying. Doing hope is one way that those who are more neurobiologically robust can share the benefits of this endowment with others who are less fortunate. It is these 'gifted' individuals who likely have the resources to imagine hope for those whose resources are depleted, leaving them hopeless.

Conclusion

In *Disturbing the Peace*, Václav Havel says of hope that it is 'definitely not the same thing as optimism. It is not the conviction that something will turn out well, but the certainty that something makes sense, regardless of how it turns out' (1991: 181). I like this distinction a great deal because it is precisely the activity of making sense of what life deals us that people do so well with each other, and that we as therapists are so skilled at doing.

His sentiment also orients us toward an appreciation of why hopeful people, as opposed to optimistic ones, may also feel discouraged or despairing. Hope is a process of arriving at a goal – no matter how much it has shifted – and making sense of the journey there. As long as despair doesn't descend into isolation, devolve into indifference or foster fear and hatred, it is just another feeling that may accompany us along our path.

Nor does false hope have a place within this conceptualization. False hope refers to pinning our expectations on an outcome that is unlikely to come true. On the other hand people do hope – in the three ways I am now conceptualizing it – all the time even though the outcome is uncertain. As Leonard Woolf (1989) said, quoting Montaigne, it is not the arrival but the journey that matters.

More worrisome is not stepping on a path at all. The other day, I was giving a workshop on 'International Work at Home: Creating Global Communities'. About half of the participants described themselves as 'ambivalent' about projects that they had considered doing, each in his or her own way fearing that in the end whatever they did do would be insignificant.

I have encountered this sentiment many times before, in myself and with other workshop participants. Yet I have come to believe that the absence of action born of deep caring shows up in the world no differently from inaction due to indifference. Older, diverted from larger projects to ones I can do with less energy, I have had to embrace the belief that small actions matter and ripple out in ways that we can never predict.

In the fall of 2003, I learned this lesson again painfully. Poised to go on a book tour for *Common Shock: Witnessing Violence Every Day: How We Are Harmed, How We Can Heal* (Weingarten 2003), instead, diagnosed with cancer, I was changing surgical dressings every 20 minutes and lying on a freezing-cold, steel radiation table. Diminished, exhausted, I was desperate to continue my work. On World AIDS Day, listening to a lecture, I realized that I could dedicate what I had – my radiation treatments – to my friends and colleagues in South Africa working with people who suffer from AIDS, their families and caregivers.

From then on, each day, I dedicated my treatment to a person or a cause whose work in relation to violence I wished to honor. I hoped that the knowledge that someone cared enough about the work they were doing to dedicate their treatment to them would encourage them in the daily challenges they faced. Dedicating my treatments brought me in virtual contact with people and organizations whose work sustained me while I was doing hope in the bowels of a hospital (Weingarten 2004, 2005).

And I felt better. Hope is a resource. We hoard it at our peril. The effects of hope are profound, as are the effects of hopelessness. It is a human rights issue. Just as food, water, and security must be equitably distributed, so, too, must hope. Whether we offer or receive, co-create or imagine, we can all participate in doing hope.

References

Bar-Tal, D. (2001) Why does fear override hope in societies engulfed by intractable conflict, as it does in Israeli society? *Political Psychology*, 22(3): 601–27.

Berry, W. (2002) Solving for pattern, in *The Art of the Commonplace*. Washington, DC: Counterpoint.

Charney, D.S. (2004) Psychobiological mechanisms of resilience and vulnerability: implications for successful adaptation to extreme stress, *The American Journal of Psychiatry*, 161(2): 195–216.

Davidson, R.J. (2003) Affective neuroscience and psychophysiology: toward a synthesis, *Psychophysiology*, 40(5): 655–65.

Groopman, J. (2004) *The Anatomy of Hope*. New York: Random House.

Hanh, T.N. (1999) *The Heart of the Buddha's Teaching*. New York: Broadway Books.

Havel, V. (1991) *Disturbing the Peace*. New York: Vintage.

Penn, P. (2001) Chronic illness: trauma, language, and writing: breaking the silence, *Family Process*, 40(1): 33–52.

Rizzolatti, G. and Craighero, L. (2004) The mirror-neuron system, *Annual Review Neuroscience*, 27: 167–92.

Sachs, J.D. (2004) Letter from Sauri, Kenya, www.worldagroforestry.org/Uploaded Documents/sauri-letter.pdf (accessed 9 August 2004).

Snyder, C.R., Sympson, S.C., Ybasco, F.C., Borders, T.F., Babyak, M.A. and Higgins, R.L. (1996) Development and validation of the State Hope Scale, *Journal of Personality and Social Psychology*, 2: 321–35.

Snyder, C.R., McDermott, D., Cook, W. and Rapoff, M. (1997) *Hope for the Journey: Helping Children through the Good Times and the Bad*. Boulder, CO: Westview.

Snyder, C.R., Cheavans, J. and Michael, S.T. (1999) Hoping, in C.R. Snyder (ed.) *Coping: The Psychology of What Works*. New York: Oxford University Press.

Tomm, K. (1997) Workshop on recent developments in family therapy, Cambridge, MA, 9 May, 1997.

Weingarten, K. (2000) Witnessing, wonder, and hope, *Family Process*, 39(4): 389–402.

Weingarten, K. (2003) *Common Shock: Witnessing Violence Every Day: How We Are Harmed, How We Can Heal*. New York: Dutton.

Weingarten, K. (2004) The ripple effect, *Hope Magazine*, 44: 34–7.

Weingarten, K. (2005) Treatment dedication guides, www.witnessingproject.org/treatded.html.

Weingarten, V. (1978) *Intimations of Mortality*. New York: Knopf.

Whitehead, A.N. (2004) Body and spirit, www.mountainman.com.au/whiteh_3.htm (accessed 12 December 2004).

Woolf, L.S. (1989) *Journey Not the Arrival Matters: An Autobiography of the Years 1939 to 1969*. New York: Harvest/HBJ.

Chapter 2

The balance of hope and hopelessness

Carmel Flaskas

Introduction

This chapter offers a set of reflections on the experience of hope and hopelessness. I am interested in thinking about individuals' and families' experience of hope and hopelessness. I am also interested in thinking about therapists' engagements with their clients' experience, as well as their own experience.

The introduction to this book noted the empirical evidence of the significance of clients' capacity for hope in the process of change. That this factor possibly accounts for as much as 15 per cent of the factors related to positive outcome in therapy, equal to the influence of the therapist's choice of particular therapeutic techniques, resonates strongly with practice impressions and also resonates strongly with themes presented in supervision.

It would be remiss not to acknowledge here, at the outset, the richness of the therapist's own relationship to hope. Separate from the issue of the sensitivity of our response to our clients' experience, we all have a personal relationship to hope, and have been drawn to the pleasures and challenges of therapeutic work. In many ways, the 'frame' of psychotherapy is itself a frame of hope in the human capacity for change. Yet therapeutic work calls on us to witness depths of sadness, loss, vulnerability, trauma, abuse, injustice, oppression, bad luck and sheer bloody tragedy alongside strength, humour, resilience, gifts, love, creativity and inspiration. That all therapists have some story to tell about their personal experience of these coexisting human polarities perhaps goes without saying. Therefore, it is unwise to write ourselves out of the picture when we are trying to understand the movable and changing scene of hope and hopelessness in work with clients.

This chapter will lay out four sets of ideas about hope and hopelessness in the context of therapy. The first is about the necessary coexistence of hope and hopelessness, and the second addresses the intimacy and power of hope and hopelessness as a layered experience of emotion, meaning and behaviour. The third set of themes concerns the relational and social context of hope and hopelessness, while the fourth directly considers the therapeutic relationship and the therapeutic use of self. As the chapter is driven strongly by my practice experience, I will include some snapshots of practice as I develop the discussion that is nonetheless primarily about ideas.

The coexistence of hope and hopelessness

The languaging of 'hope' and 'hopelessness' invokes an oppositional polarity, for 'hope' is counterposed by its own lack – 'hopelessness'. In this way, an either/or relationship is deeply embedded in the language that we have available to use when we try to address this aspect of human experience. However, despite the polarity of the language of hope, it is very rare to experience a state of unbounded hope. Unfortunately, it is much easier to imagine (or remember) the opposite polarity – an experience where hopelessness feels unbounded. Here, the word 'despair' may be invoked to describe those times in which the possibility of feeling hope or being hopeful is eclipsed by a totalizing sense of hopelessness.

The argument that hope and hopelessness are not either/or experiences is made very powerfully in one of the few family therapy discussions of this topic. Amaryll Perlesz (1999) teases out the relationship through reflection on her own personal experience, her practice and her empirical research. She locates her personal context as a child and grandchild of Holocaust survivors, and the resonances with her professional experience of working with families where one person has sustained a head injury. Her empirical research with these families negated the expected corollary between personal and family strengths on the one hand, and levels of distress and dissatisfaction on the other. Greater strengths did not necessarily relate to less distress and less dissatisfaction in living with the aftermath of one member of the family sustaining a head injury.

Perlesz gives a description from practice that illustrates this unexpected finding. As the therapy and time progresses, a woman shows remarkable courage and resilience in her capacity to grieve the husband she has lost to head injury, and to find the ability to relate to, and love, the husband she still has. Alongside her journey, there is a parallel movement for her husband in his relationship to himself, his wife and his children. It is certainly an illustration of great strength and hope, but Perlesz notes that to tell only this part of the story gives just a piecemeal description of the woman's experience as, several years later, she is still testing in the clinical range for depression. One conclusion that is drawn is that the depression speaks to the ongoing realness of the tragedy and loss, which is not lessened by the strength of the capacity for resilience and transformation, but instead sits side-by-side, speaking to the complexity of the human response to trauma.

When reading this article, I was curious that, although I found the results of the empirical research surprising, I was moved, but not at all surprised, by the practice illustration. My sense of this contradiction in my expectations of empirical and clinical knowledge is this. While I am influenced by the dichotomous thinking embedded in the languaging of hope and hopelessness and the professional discourse that spins off from this, at another level I have a practice knowledge that challenges this dichotomous thinking. As therapists, most of us 'know' from our personal and professional experience that hope and hopelessness exist in complex relationship. The very difficult human experiences of loss, abuse, trauma and tragedy often call forth simultaneously the equal 'extremes' of an inspired response of hope, courage and resilience, as well as great pain and an ongoing deep sense of hopelessness which may, or may not, be mediated by time.

Thus, we have a strong practice knowledge that hope and hopelessness are not 'opposite' experiences. Even to talk of a 'continuum' or 'range' of experience from hope through to hopelessness is quite misleading in this territory of human experience, for when hope is high, hopelessness is not necessarily low, and this is perhaps especially the case when facing abuse, trauma and tragedy. Thus, as Nollaig Byrne and Imelda McCarthy argue in their contribution to this book, hope and hopelessness exist in a dialectical rather than an oppositional relationship, and this is the idea that the writer and critic Nikos Papastergiadis expresses when he says: 'of course hope is the other side of despair – and being closer to one reminds you of the need for the other' (Papastergiadis in Zournazi 2002: 82).

The expression of hope and hopelessness: feeling, thinking, doing

So far I have been exploring the coexistence of hope and hopelessness, and the question of what kind of 'state' we might be talking about when we talk about the 'state' of hope and hopelessness has been put on hold. Very often, hope and hopelessness are represented and constructed in therapeutic discourse as an internal feeling state – the property, if you like, of the individual, with the emotionality of the experience being privileged. I think we ignore at our peril the powerfulness of the intimate individual emotional experience of hope and despair, not the least because the experience of hopelessness and despair is so painful and also so potentially impoverishing and destructive of self and human relationships. The peril, then, of turning our backs on the emotionality of hope and hopelessness in either our theory or our practice is that we risk creating a chasm in our empathic connection with clients and underestimating the power of the emotional experience of hope and hopelessness.

Yet to stay oriented just to the individual feeling state of hope and despair undermines the richness of the relationship of emotion, meaning and behaviour in human experience. Thus, we might feel hopeful and hopeless, have beliefs and meanings that generate and support our emotional experience, as well as do things that either nurture or undermine our capacity for hope. The state of hope and hopelessness, then, like other human states, is expressed and communicated through emotion, meaning and behaviour. Clinically we know that a unity of emotion, belief and behaviour is forceful for better or worse. It becomes 'for worse' when people feel a totalizing sense of hopelessness, have a well-developed and fixed set of beliefs about why they should be feeling this way, and are doing things in their lives and relationships which are more likely to strengthen the power of despair and provide ongoing evidence of its 'reasons'. It becomes 'for better' when a counterbalancing hope emerges in all three spheres of feeling, meaning and behaviour.

Clinically we also know that a leeway for therapeutic change often lies in people's capacity to mobilize change by actively using the disparity in their feeling, meaning and behaviour:

'I know,' says a father in the presence of his teenage daughter who has significant drug abuse, 'that we should just give up here, and that it is looking very bad, but I still just feel that somewhere somehow she really knows who she is and that we are behind her, and we will all get through this.'

A woman who has endured many losses, whose own mother had serious depression, and is vulnerable herself to depression and anxiety, describes continuing to hold her small baby boy closely and gently to her breast while battling hopelessness and a sudden intense urge to push him away.

'Fake it till you make it' a saying reported from a Narcotics Anonymous group.

These snapshots circle the final idea in this set of themes: that there may be different expressions and communications in the feeling, thinking and doing of hope and hopelessness. In Kaethe Weingarten's words, you can 'do' hope even when you can't feel hope (Weingarten 2000). The capacity to feel hope, even when there seems no rational meaning to support this hope, can be witnessed and honoured by significant others and in the therapeutic environment. Moreover, through the painstaking work of reflection and restorying – which is primarily aimed at changing meaning – it is possible to work toward the discovery and creation of more hopeful stories. In short, in the process of change, the differences in feeling, thinking and doing hope can be actively used to challenge and shift the balance of hope and hopelessness.

The social and relational context of hope and hopelessness

Exploring the relational and social context of the experience of hope and hopelessness is the next step in this chapter. Kaethe Weingarten (2000) has written not just of the idea of the importance of 'doing' hope in her reflections on the process of hope. Just as strongly, she has emphasized the relational context of hope, which is further developed in her contribution to this book. In an article that was originally written as a presentation at a conference in South Africa, Weingarten weaves a discussion addressing the political context of hope, the community context of (and responsibility for) hope, and the intimacy of the individual and family experience of hope. Like Perlesz, she holds her own life experiences directly alongside her practice experience. In talking with a woman who feels deeply hopeless in the face of secondary cancer, she says: 'Of course you feel hopeless. It is not your job right now to feel hope. Rather, it is the responsibility of others who love you to *do hope* with you' (italics in original); Weingarten then concludes strongly that 'hope is something we do with others' (Weingarten 2000: 402).

The relational context of hope and hopelessness, then, may involve the family constellation around hope, the community context and the extent to which this context can support hope, as well as bearing in mind the broader political context and the way in which this constructs or undermines the individual and family and community experiences of hope. In the territory of therapy, we also need to factor ourselves in as therapists and the part that the therapeutic relationship and environment can play in the balance of hope and hopelessness.

In thinking first about family constellations around hope, I will note the way in which hope and hopelessness are often 'divvied up' between family members, and 'held' by the family as a whole. One sees this more clearly when times are fraught and something very important is seen to be at stake. For example, one parent may 'hold' the hope for a child facing a life-threatening illness or a painful and degenerative disability, while the other parent may hold the fear and hopelessness about the outcome. Sometimes, this pattern of division is quite fixed, matching the parents' different capacities for nurturing hope and tolerating hopelessness, capacities which are often grounded in intergenerational and life histories. Other times, the divvying up is more fluid, as if at a subliminal level the partners pick up on each other's thresholds for holding hope or hopelessness, and somehow they periodically 'swap' positions.

The other divvying up one sees between different family members is in the communication and expression of hope and hopelessness through emotion, meaning and behaviour. To follow the example, one parent may feel hopeless and 'think' despair, yet consistently and unambivalently 'do' hope for the child. The other parent may hold onto the capacity to language and 'think' and feel hope for the child and for the family, yet find it harder to do the daily activities and labours of hope that come with the territory of a sick child.

I have been using this example simply as a beginning illustration of the kind of division of hope and hopelessness that happens within families. The fuller map of family relationships is broader in the way in which family members step in and out of hope and hopelessness in relation to each other, and also shift across the feeling, thinking and doing of hope. Of course, we use the word 'family' always as a shorthand to indicate the network and connections-across-time of intimate relationships. Thus, though in therapy we are often working with the immediate and very intimate nuclear family relationships, the map of the wider family distribution of hope and hopelessness is much wider. It may include parents and partners and children, brothers and sisters, aunties and uncles, grandparents and great-grandparents, the intimacy of friendships-across-time, and families-of-choice. There are also the legacies that are carried about hope and despair from those important others who have died but are nonetheless still held very much in the minds of those who continue to live.

Involvement in community memberships also changes the equation of hope and hopelessness. The literature on family resilience (see for example Walsh 1998) and strengths-based practice approaches (see for example De Jong and Miller 1995; Saleeby 1996) alerts us to something we 'know' but can easily downplay in the immediacy of the comparatively narrow focus of clinical work: people have multiple community memberships, including memberships and identifications associated with culture or race or religion or class, with schools and workplaces, and within the patterns of everyday social connectedness. These multiple memberships across the family potentially throw a wider net of support for hope and hopefulness, and also sometimes embed hopelessness. The daily grind of poverty, the locality of hopelessness in some big public housing estates, the current and historical experiences of some communities of stigma, discrimination and injustice, intergenerational experiences of family abuse – all these possibilities, which are not mutually exclusive, can make it much harder for individuals and families to hold the balance of hope and hopelessness in favour of hope.

I have been remembering a family I've written about before, though I was not then thinking explicitly about the centrality of hope and hopelessness.[1] An 8-year-old boy, with his auntie and cousin, are referred by an Aboriginal service following a suicidal enactment. Bit-by-bit, different layers unfold as we meet – his experience of racism at school; his difficulty in belonging, either culturally or in his family (he does not look Aboriginal, unlike his auntie and cousin); and his loss of his mother who had left him with his auntie because she had a problem with drinking and could not look after him. The boy doesn't seem unhappy, yet he has carried out an act of despair, all the more worrying because it seems so unattached to language and conscious meaning. I worried for him then, and I worry for him now, and my fantasy/fear is that he could end up suiciding in later life. I also know that this is a 'worst' fear and it may not happen, and that there are many factors that point toward his moving through this.

I cannot not know the political and historical context of this boy's struggle with life, and sit as a white Australian therapist hearing his auntie tell his mother's story of being removed from her family as part of the stolen generation, and her understanding of the effects for her sister. The issue of belonging, and the boy's lack of hope about belonging, is only too intimately and personally experienced in the here-and-now and yet firmly grounded in the realness and history of political oppression and intergenerational and cultural pain. However, in the balance of hope and hopelessness that is going on, his auntie mobilizes the forces. She feels and does hope for him at a point when he has not learnt to do it for himself, and the network of support for hope widens as some important other people in his family and community get involved, his teacher and school respond, and the therapy environment becomes part of this network as well. I am not sure how the balance will fall for this boy, though I can see the power of the social and relational context of hope and hopelessness, for good and ill.

The therapeutic relationship and the therapist's use of self

I have just been arguing for an appreciation of the layering of the relational and social context of hope and hopelessness for individuals and families, and the extent to which the dynamics of these contexts can act as a resource or restraint for both hopefulness and the capacity to tolerate and balance hopelessness. This appreciation offers a set of compass points in our reflections and our conversations with families. However, to have access to compass points around the dynamics of hope and hopelessness is important not just for thinking about the family's experience, but also for thinking about our own experience as therapists in the therapeutic relationship. To quote again from the introduction to this book, the research on generic factors associated with positive outcomes in therapy suggests that of the factors associated with what we as therapists have to offer in therapy, the therapeutic relationship continues to be the single most important ingredient, weighing in at twice the significance of particular techniques or models of therapy.

Thankfully, as therapists we cannot help but be involved with patterns of hope and hopelessness in our work with clients. The psychoanalyst Stephen

Mitchell could easily be addressing psychotherapy in general when he writes: 'the analyst's hopes for her patients are embedded in and deeply entangled with her own sense of herself, her worth, what she can offer, what she has found deeply meaningful in her own life . . . our hopes for the patient are inextricably bound up with our hopes for ourselves' (1993: 208). Indeed, our capacity to allow our 'selves' to be put at the service of, and used by, our clients accounts for a large part of the potential richness of the therapeutic relationship, and also accounts for a lot of its messiness.

From the beginning of our engagement with families, we have reactions to and resonances with their relationships to hope and hopelessness. Sometimes, we find ourselves understanding one person's expressions of hope and hopelessness more easily, and this affects our capacity to appreciate the integrity of the family's distribution of hope. To appreciate this integrity does not preclude our staying alert to the way in which the distribution may be experienced as unfair by some family members, or may be fanning a painful aloneness for particular family members, or may be steadily corroding a sense of emotional connectedness in the family as a whole.

Sometimes it is easy to find ourselves being silently critical of what appears to be an overbalance of hope in a family where very real and serious issues are at stake. We give up our curiosity to think about this disparity, and we trade in our capacity for an empathic stance toward the family's struggle that has come to show itself this way. In still other situations, where families present with what seems like an overbalance of hopelessness in proportion to their description of their struggles, it can be hard to resist either covertly or overtly trying to talk them out of their hopelessness. Again, both the capacity for curiosity about the family's expression of hopelessness and the capacity for empathy are compromised.

However, the most challenging time for therapists is often in periods of impasse, when the therapeutic work becomes stuck, and the fear and expectation of failure can set in with a vengeance for both family and therapist. I have written before (Flaskas 2002, 2005) about the way in which intense feelings of despair, anger, blame and shame often trigger 'anti-therapeutic sequences' in the therapeutic relationship during impasse, and the capacity of both the family and the therapist to hope for something better is undermined. It can be important at times like these to hold hope for the family, including the hope that the feelings of hopelessness and the fear of failure will become more bearable.

In some ways, as therapists we 'do' a version of what family members do for each other, which is the emotional equivalent of putting up your hand and offering to temporarily hold hope for others – and, like family members, we have various possibilities for feeling, thinking and/or doing hope in our work. However, precisely because as therapists we have our own personal relationships to hope and hopelessness, as well as particular hopes for each family we work with, the task is to hold on to a therapeutic position that stays other-focused while using our 'self' as fully as possible as a resource. There is nothing magical about this process, though it can be at times very difficult. The task calls for the discipline of reflection, and using what Peter Rober (1999) calls our 'inner conversations' about the family and the therapeutic process as well as 'outer conversations' with colleagues, in supervision and with the family.

Many practice situations have been floating through my head as I have written this section . . . I have been thinking of work with a number of different people who have survived early sexual abuse, and of the common period mid-therapy when the person feels overwhelmed by the awfulness of their childhood experience – the awfulness that somehow now becomes able to be known more clearly than was possible at the time. These periods of therapy are intensely painful and can be quite frightening, with suicidality and other acts of destruction lurking around. As the therapist, I struggle to hold the hope myself, to keep a steady course that stays oriented to my client's capacity for resilience, and yet to remain available to witnessing the pain and despair without either reacting against it or being swamped by it.

I have also been thinking about ongoing discussions with an adolescent mental health team with whom I meet regularly for consultation. Some of the most challenging presentations have been around situations where a young person is in an increasingly serious pattern of self-harm, mutilation and suicidality. The levels of despair and anxiety and anger skyrocket with each new act of horror, and the positioning of blame intensifies as the fear of a dead young woman burns through the system. 'The system' by now includes the young person, the parent/s, the family, the group of friends, the school counsellor and teachers, the treating psychiatrist, the staff of the ward where she was hospitalized – and in the adolescent mental health team, the primary therapist/s and everyone on the team who has been caught up in one crisis or another on intake. For the parent/s, the unbearable thought that their daughter might die often makes hope itself dangerous. Anticipatory grief sets in, which can easily look more like emotional abandonment to outsiders and be experienced as such by the young person herself. The therapist tries to hold hope in a way that is not oppositional to the family and young woman – and it can be very hard to juggle the tasks of holding hope while tolerating knowing the anxiety and despair, and staying in an open and empathic position to the family and colleagues.[2]

Conclusions

This chapter has developed four sets of ideas about hope and hopelessness. It has been an argument for acknowledging the complexity of the coexistence of hope and hopelessness in human experience; it has been an argument for the opportunities and fluidity inherent in our capacity to think, feel and do both hope and hopelessness; it has been an argument for thinking about the social and relational contexts of hope and hopelessness, and the distribution of hope and hopelessness within families and their broader contexts; and it has been an argument that as therapists we should value and attend to our engagement with hope and hopelessness in the therapeutic relationship.

All these ideas give compass points for how we might choose to orient to hope and hopelessness in our work with families. Let me use this conclusion to list and summarize some practice orientations that these ideas may offer:

- We can attend specifically to the experience of hope and hopelessness of families we work with, especially in situations of chronicity and when the anxiety of serious outcomes are at stake; and we can attend to our own experience of hope and hopelessness as therapists in the therapeutic relationship, again especially in these same situations, and in critical periods of engagement and impasse.
- We can directly invite conversations with families about their experience of hopelessness and hope.
- When we move beyond assumptions about the oppositionality of hope and hopelessness, we can move beyond the confines of the language of 'too much' hopelessness or 'too little' hope. Language that is pitched more toward the balance of hope and hopelessness, or the distribution of hope, or the network of hope, or even the quotient of hope and hopelessness, opens up different spaces in our own thinking and in the way we talk with families.
- To be attuned as therapists to the coexistence of strong hope and strong hopelessness, especially in experiences of abuse, trauma, loss and tragedy, allows us to stay open to witnessing more fully the realness of our clients' experiences.
- To 'know' that in some situations the experience of deep hopelessness cannot be cured or talked away allows us to stay more connected to our clients' experience. It also allows us to hold hope about the way in which hopelessness may come to be experienced as more tolerable across time, and the way in which the active nurturing of the feeling, thinking and doing of hope may change the quotient of hope and hopelessness. If you like, deep hopelessness can come to be mediated by strengthening hope – the balance shifts, even if the hopelessness itself stays just as strong.
- We can use the therapeutic leeway of different ways in which different

members of the family might feel, think and do hope to make more visible the labour that is being undertaken within the family. Doing this often opens out possibilities for different ways in which the labour of hope and hopelessness may be shared both within and beyond the family.

- While we orient respectfully to the sense and integrity of the family's current distribution of hope and hopelessness, a conversation about this distribution can also heighten the awareness of the effects of this distribution on different family members. This kind of conversation potentially offers a safety net in situations in which the sense of family connectedness is being undermined in more polarized distributions.
- It is useful to hold the power of the broader social and historical context in mind. This potentially guides us in our conversations with families. Moreover, it always useful to know the limits alongside valuing the capacities of the territory of therapy, as well as the capacities and limits of our place as therapists within broader therapeutic systems.

There are undoubtedly a great many ways in which we can usefully engage with the experience of hope and hopelessness in our work with families. I imagine that the compass points offered by the ideas developed here may lead to a different set of practice orientations for colleagues who work differently. But whichever way different practice orientations may lead, I will nonetheless conclude with a strong plea for theory and practice to embrace the complexity of the balance of hope and hopelessness in lived experience.

Notes

1 See Flaskas (2002), pp. 118–19 and 132–3.
2 Pam Rycroft (2004) has written a poignant reflection on her work as co-therapist with the family of a young woman who eventually suicided; many of her themes are resonant with the discussion here.

References

De Jong, P. and Miller, S. (1995) How to interview for client strengths, *Social Work*, 40(6): 729–36.
Flaskas, C. (2002) *Family Therapy Beyond Postmodernism: Practice Challenges Theory*. Hove: Brunner-Routledge.
Flaskas, C. (2005) Sticky situations, therapy mess: on impasse and reflective practice, in C. Flaskas, B. Mason and A. Perlesz (eds) *The Space Between: Experience, Context and Process in the Therapeutic Relationship*. London: Karnac Books.
Mitchell, S. A. (1993) *Hope and Dread in Psychoanalysis*. New York: Basic Books.
Perlesz, A. (1999) Complex responses to trauma: challenges in bearing witness, *Australian and New Zealand Journal of Family Therapy*, 20(1): 11–19.
Rober, P. (1999) The therapist's inner conversation in family therapy practice: some ideas about the self of the therapist, therapeutic impasse and the process of reflection, *Family Process*, 38(2): 209–28.

Rycroft, P. (2004) When theory abandons us – wading through the 'swampy lowlands' of practice, *Journal of Family Therapy*, 26(3): 245–59.

Saleeby, D. (1996) The strengths perspective in social work practice: extensions and cautions, *Social Work*, 41(3): 296–305.

Walsh, F. (1998) *Strengthening Family Resilience*. New York: Guilford.

Weingarten, K. (2000) Witnessing, wonder and hope, *Family Process*, 39(4): 389–402.

Zournazi, M. (2002) Faith without certitudes – with Nikos Papastergiadis, in *Hope: New Philosophies for Change*. Sydney: Pluto Press Australia.

Chapter 3

The dialectical structure of hope and despair: a Fifth Province Approach

Nollaig Byrne and Imelda McCarthy

> Hope consists in asserting that there is at the heart of being, beyond all
> data, beyond all inventories and all calculations a mysterious principle
> which is in connivance with me.
>
> (Marcel 1995: 28)

Introduction

From the antique period, through to the age 'of conversion' and into medieval
times the figures of Justice and Injustice, Truth and Falsehood, Love and
Hatred, Hope and Despair have been visually elaborated as opposing personifications. They form pairs in the Virtue–Vice cycle in which struggle and
overcoming posit a type of religious attitude. The figures of Hope and Despair are both related to the future, one redeemed, one doomed, an afterlife of
either heaven or hell (Barash 1999). However, at the heart of this struggle is
the maintenance of an unbounded hope with the expectancy of an eternal life.

From the trajectory of western Enlightenment, progressive secularization
and the Marxist ideal, the dream world of human possibility is represented as
the substitute for a religious-type afterlife but has retained a similar oppositional structure of struggle and overcoming. In this trajectory the question
of oppression–emancipation as a dialectical opposition is still driven by a
politics of hope but now oriented to the secular variant of utopia and the
universal human good.

In the contemporary understanding a 'privatization of hope' arrives on
the agenda replacing the profound hopefulness which had animated the
twentieth-century socialist vision. This is the Fukuyama (1992) conception of
a society without opposition, no longer requiring large theoretical schemata
of emancipation. Rather it is populated by an infinity of individual hopes and
partial social projects (Anderson 1992). While this speaks to the modern
heterogeneity of being and a politics of gradualism, it fails to account for the
engagement with the world, revealing hope in the bleakest situations, or its
opposite, the wish for death in the withdrawal of despair.

Hope and despair: from the classical-Christian to the secular imaginations

In the Christian imagination of the Middle Ages the allegorical figure of Despair (*Desperatio*) was transferred to the historical Judas, represented by Judas hanging from a tree, and sometimes juxtaposed with the crucified Jesus, the Christian figure of Hope (Barash 1999). While church iconography continued to include the pairing of virtues and vices in classical allegorical personifications, virtues, those divine and those developed through human effort, were no longer cast as oppositions. However, Despair continued as the contrasting figure denoting absence of Hope.

The tradition of secular hope initiated by the Enlightenment is a revaluation of human capacities to discern, to will, to judge, to imagine and to hope. The three questions founding Kant's critique of reason are, 'What can I know? What should I do? For what can I hope?' (Kant 1961: 645). Here the religious impulse is now directed to interests of the world with a privileged rationality as the backbone for moral development. In this tradition the object of hope is humanity itself with more self-knowledge, more freedom and more material progress. However, the intention here is to articulate human freedom while maintaining the place of religious belief or a spiritual orientation to the world.

Communism, the 'New Faith' in a utopian world, shifted the geography and timescale of transcendent hope to a world created by man's efforts. The hoped-for transcendent perfection of a classless society with no division of labour and control of nature through technology promised to fulfil man's deepest yearning for a good life: 'Once he has grasped himself and established what is his, without expropriation and alienation in real democracy, there arises in the world something which shines into the childhood of all in which no one has yet been: homeland' (Bloch 1986: 1375–6).

Despair is the appropriate marker for the collapse of the greatest secular hope of our time, the utopian socialist vision laid waste by the crimes carried out in its name (Milosz 2001). From this wasteland of politics without opposition, the 'social hopes' of Rorty and Fukuyama, commentators from the Left and Right respectively, exemplify optimism as the emotional fluency of subjects in liberal democratic societies; polities that guarantee the well-being of individuals under conditions of liberty and freedom – the realization of 'the democratic ideal'. Here the future is foreclosed, requiring only optimism and a deflection of imagining how things might be otherwise, thus rendering hope of salvation, be it political or religious, both obsolete and archaic. This society has been achieved through man's efforts and optimism and only requires for its sustenance a trust in progress and growth. In this depiction hope and the social relation it evokes is suppressed and optimism is unbounded (Lasch 1991). Rorty counters this unboundedness with a moderated optimism and a place for 'small experimental ways' to replace grand projects (1998: 228).

In our present understanding we borrow vestiges from religious and secular traditions to account for occasions of hope and despair. Yet it is from the great failures of modern times, particularly in the twentieth century, that we draw to moderate and guide our response. It is the events of evil and suffering in our time nearing apocalyptic proportions, the Holocaust, the gulags, wars and genocide, famines and natural catastrophes that create the ground for embracing despair, for persevering in the face of tragedy and hoping for hope. These crisis situations highlight basic trust, the social relation and community as the place of hope. It is the ground where the possibility of the social relation is revealed as the place of hope. Likewise Camus, when referring to writing *The Plague*, said, 'If there is one fact that these last five years have brought out, it is the extreme solidarity of men with one another' (Camus 1968: 346).

The Fifth Province[1]

The Fifth Province is a therapeutic approach that provides a systemic analysis from a dialectical vantage point. In a Fifth Province application the movement of hope and despair is held in dramatic tension. They are not oppositions to be overcome, a hierarchy to be reversed or an unfolding synthesis. Rather they are discursive identities with an immeasurable hiatus, which seek reconciliation with each other, not evaluation. It is this oscillating condition of hiatus and reconciliation that positions the endurance of hope and the closure of despair as a conjoined future perspective. Creating the circumstances for therapeutic hope thus requires an acknowledgement of, and an understanding of, clients' horizons of meaning together with the moral, political and more personal sources which animate them.

From a Fifth Province point of view what we attempt to do is to co-create a therapeutic space – in mind, conversation and relationship – that invites ambivalence and resists the impulse toward categorical impositions.[2]

Clinical vignette: an archetype of despair

A Child Protection team sought a consultation with us, the authors, for Patrick and Anne, a couple in their late twenties with five children, aged between 9 years and 3 months. Two months prior to the sessions outlined below, Anne had tried to smother her youngest child, Michael, by placing a pillow over his face while he slept. He was rushed to the accident and emergency department of a children's hospital and was detained. At the hospital, the medical staff assumed that he had experienced an apnoeic episode, 'a case of near cot death'. Later Anne, in a distraught state, attended her GP and disclosed to him what she had done. He immediately advised her to inform her husband and the hospital, and also made a report to the Child Protection Services. On discharge from the hospital Michael was placed in foster care while a risk assessment was carried out. Initially, Patrick was reluctant to cooperate with social services, saying that he 'wanted to forget the event, put things right and have Michael home'. The Child Protection team had concerns about Patrick's under-response to such a grave event and his apparent unwillingness to cooperate in a parental and risk assessment. Anne was referred for psychiatric evaluation, received a diagnosis of post-natal depression and was prescribed medication.

The event, the mother's attempt to kill her infant, is the crisis threatening both the dispersal of the family and the disintegration of parental roles. However, this significance is marginalized by the professional attempt to establish risk and by the parents' own attempt to exit emotionally from the scene of despair. Using 'questioning at the extremes' (Colgan 1991) the catastrophic scene is addressed within an 'as if' future frame. This frame was prompted by Anne's 'as if' assumptions that her baby was the cause of her problems.

The participants in the excerpted interview reproduced below include the parents, Anne and Patrick, the social worker team, Tom and Mary, and the Fifth Province team composed of the authors.

'If he wasn't there': despair as the unwanted child

Imelda (to Anne)	So when you became aware of the eviction threat, and you made the decision to kill Michael, what was in your mind at that time? Was it to get Patrick's attention, to solve the housing problem or to call attention to yourself? Like, who or what was most on your mind?
Patrick:	I wouldn't say she consciously made the decision to kill Michael.
Imelda:	You had some sort of a plan of killing the baby, is that right?
Anne:	No, I had said to myself, *if* he wasn't there. I didn't actually plan to get rid of him but I had focused it on him. You see Patrick and I had had a row and he had said that he was my responsibility, so I think I felt that *if* he wasn't there I wouldn't be having all these problems and the particular reason that morning I was saying to myself, *if* Michael wasn't there none of this would happen but it wasn't a conscious thing, you know, 'I'll kill him', it was more the fact that *if* I hadn't had him, *if* he wasn't there . . .

The event has drawn stark attention to the infant's unwanted status. In this short sequence two other movements are brought forth by the couple. Patrick's answering for Anne was a protective (if minimizing) move while Anne invites a speculative view of the past through her words, 'if Michael wasn't there, none of this would happen'. Noting this, the interviewer takes the thread of a speculative past and juxtaposes it with a speculative future.

The fantasy of revenge

Imelda: If you had succeeded in killing Michael how do you think Patrick would have reacted?

Anne: It is difficult to say. At that particular time I think it would have finished us *(looks at husband)* totally and completely.

Imelda: Would he have killed you?

Anne: I don't know. I couldn't answer that myself. You would have to ask him.

Imelda: What is your belief about it?
(to
Patrick)

Patrick: I would sooner not think about it. I would like to put it behind us. It's gone.

Imelda: What is your worst fear about what you might have done?

Patrick: Kill her. I have a temper, a bad temper but I never take it out on Anne or the kids.

While having the form of an evasive reply, it is also likely that Patrick's fantasy of revenge was sufficiently present to make it threatening. His statement, 'It's gone', points to an experience of desperation overcome and a hope to be held. However, knowing that this kind of hope living in the space of denial would alarm the social workers, the field of reflection was expanded and Social Services were now included in the 'as if' scenario. The juxtaposing of past and future, reality and imagination, desperation and hope intensifies the dilemma of denial and acknowledgement. Knowing from past experiences that the denial or minimization of serious child welfare issues fuels professional fears it was important to reflect on the parents' perceptions of professional concern at this juncture.

Loss, despair and the emergence of hope

Imelda: Could I ask you what do you think the Health Board (Social Services) would have done?

Anne: If Michael had died? Well I suppose they would have taken the others. I don't really know.

Imelda: And how would that have been? If they had come in to protect the other children, would that have left you on your own without Patrick or do you think Patrick would have moved back to be with you or would he have kept away?

Anne: I think possibly he would have stayed away.

Imelda: Do you agree with that, Patrick?

Patrick: No! If they had moved in to take the kids? If the worst had come to the worst and Michael had died, I would have told Anne to go back to her mother and I would have kept the kids. I would have organized somebody, my mother or somebody in the family, to look after the kids while I was at work. There is no way that I would have let the family go.

Imelda: OK, you would have asked Anne to leave, but you would have kept the kids.

Patrick: If the worst had come to the worst I would have kept the children together and told Anne to go back to her mother's maybe for a couple of years or five or six years or however long it would take.

Imelda: And would you have kept contact with Anne?

Patrick: Ah yeah. I can't say I would not have kept contact.

Imelda: And would you let her see the kids?

Patrick: Yeah. You never can take a mother away from her children.

Anne as the perpetrator is the melancholy figure in the tragedy that has squandered her hopes. Patrick's 'No!' is a refusal or resistance to this and allows him to hope in the transcendent values he places on family and motherhood: 'You never can take a mother away from her children.' Whilst he would protect the family unit he would nevertheless maintain Anne's status as mother. Once again working at the extremes of the 'as if' situation, the expanded field was remembered as a vantage point for the father's self-review. In this expanded field, glimpses now emerge of parental responsibility for the future care and protection of Michael. It is the beginning of a co-created space in which the voices of parental responsibility can begin to sound.

An acknowledgement story

Imelda: And how do you think the Health Board would have responded? How do you think the Health Board would have viewed you as 'Dad'? Do you think they would have supported you in that? What is your view?

Patrick: Well, talking to the senior social worker I don't think they would have. Because they believe there is a problem with me as well. It is true I was blind for two years and did not see what was going on. I know where I went wrong for the last couple of years. I have looked at myself and the way things were between us for the last twelve months or two years. I mean it is two years of my life I want to forget.

Imelda: And in wanting to forget, because in some ways coming to a place like this is about remembering, how would that be?

Patrick: Well, it is very hard, especially if there are some things that you just don't want to remember, that you want to put out of your mind and say it is gone. It is really very difficult.

Imelda: Anne, how do you think it would be for Patrick, who really wants to put this behind him, forget about it and move on and to rebuild your lives together, to come to a place like this where we are asking you to remember quite painful, quite difficult things?

Anne: Well, I think it would be very hard because Patrick doesn't like to talk about things concerning us, outside the family. I think that is difficult and like that too, it is difficult to talk about the things maybe you don't really want to talk about.

Imelda: Do you think he could do it?

Anne: Ah yeah.

Imelda: Do you think he will do it?

Anne: Yeah.

Patrick: Yeah.

Imelda: Will he do it more for himself, for you or for the children?

> Patrick continues his engendering of hope for Anne. He can begin to acknowledge his own failures as husband and father. 'It is true I was blind for two years and did not see what was going on.' In these words he is attempting to create the solidarity and bonding in their relationship from which hope might emerge. This is a first step in paternal reinstatement. The hope that Michael could come home becomes the redemptive possibility for a fractured family as Patrick engages with the reality of Anne's despair.

Truth as grounds for hope: motherhood re-imagined

Patrick: The first point is that no one would have known about it only for Anne had said it. The hospital wasn't aware. It was a case of a near cot death and they weren't aware of the situation until a week later when Anne told them.

Imelda: OK. But here you have a very serious act that Anne did while depressed and then she told the GP about it. But say the courts were not willing to take the risk of returning a small child at that point . . .

Patrick: It is possible, yeah.

Imelda: OK. How is that going to be for you two as parents?

Anne: Em . . . I would be very upset, of course, but even knowing that there was a possibility they would not send him home I still think that we would be prepared to fight it because I think he is ready to come home. I am most certainly ready for him, so even though we know that there would be a chance we would fail, we would still go ahead.

Patrick: We would know we would have done something, instead of just letting it go.

Imelda: And would you be doing that more for yourself or for Michael in the future, so that he could say, well, his parents had fought for him, they had not abandoned him?

Anne: No, for all of us.

Patrick: We would be doing it for all of us. For Michael and for all of the children, for Anne and myself, because I think the sooner the better that we can get ourselves back together, the better.

Anne: As long as Michael is with his foster mother . . . em . . . I cannot put it behind me and start to go on. It is constant . . .

Patrick: We don't want to sweep it under the carpet.

Anne: I am not going to sweep it under the carpet and pretend it didn't happen but I can't go ahead with the rest of my life until I have Michael home and have the family together. I think when I do have him home then I can go ahead. I have learned a lot from what happened. Even if they do let him come home and Tom and Mary still feel there is a need for us to come we would still be prepared, even if he did come home. We wouldn't say that we would not have to do any more, we would still be prepared, and if there was anything else we had to do. I mean we would still go ahead and do it.

Imelda: Do you think Patrick would agree with that?

Anne: Yeah. *(Both look at each other)*

Patrick: Not just for the Health Board . . .

Anne: It would be for us as well.

Patrick: From our point of view as well we would do it.

Anne: Em . . . I mean when I went to see my own doctor [GP] at the time and I told him what happened, he said he would have to notify the Health Board and I did not want that and he said, 'Well, the way it is Anne, there is no point in something like this happening and you not learning from it' and I still feel that and for the two of us, as people and for the family . . . If there was anything else we could do that would maybe improve our life, our marriage, because I mean we don't want to turn around, maybe in a year or two years and everything to fall to pieces. So, you know, if Mary and Tom said, 'Well, OK, he can come home but we still think you should attend wherever'. So, even if the outcome came in our favour I would still go on the recommendations that the Health Board had. I mean we want Michael back.

> Anne disclosed her secret without coercion one week after the event. Without intending it to be so, much as her attempt to kill the baby had not been intended, the disclosure exceeded the bounds of a confessional narrative to become a redemptive act. It opened the way, not yet for hope but for self-recognition and the recognition due to her from others. Working at the extremes of their situation, the father's commitment to his children's safety and to his family emerges ever more strongly. A new and stronger configuration of parenthood emerges as the conversation continues.

'Whatever it would take': hope as perseverance

Imelda: OK and this is the worst scenario I am painting so, you did not win your fight for your son, what would you think would be a likely way you would handle that, because these are the questions that the people in the court will be asking.

Anne: Yeah . . . em. Well it is hard to say, we would do whatever it would take.

Patrick: The first time I was here I said I would move heaven and earth to get him back. We just want him back.

Anne: If we lost the court case and we had to do further therapy we would do it. We would do whatever it takes to get him home.

Imelda: OK, let me ask you something. Patrick is saying he will move
(to   heaven and earth to have Michael back and that if he thought he
Anne)   was going to lose Michael that he would keep the children as a family unit. That was one of the things he mentioned the last day. *(Anne nods.)*

Anne: That was only if we thought we were going to lose Michael permanently.

Patrick: That is the worst thing.

Imelda: Yeah, that is what we are looking at. Patrick was saying he would let you go in order to keep the family together.

Anne: If I thought myself that Michael was going to be placed in care permanently, that we would never get him back and there was a possibility that his foster mother would get custody of him, I would sooner he was with Patrick and the other children, his family, than he being placed in care.

Imelda: So you would make that sacrifice. It would not be only Patrick who was saying 'to have this family unit together, for the kids . . . we'll have to provide a safe place'. You would also be part of that.

Anne: I would be more prepared, I think, myself to know he was safe with him and his brothers and sisters than he was in care forever.

Patrick and Anne do not know what lies ahead of them. He 'will move heaven and earth' as a sign of his perseverance. Anne will do whatever is required including sacrificing her place in the family to secure Michael's membership there. This is the recovery of hope for Michael that did not accompany his birth. Here is the rebirth of a jointly committed parenthood. The more they are questioned at the extremes of their own dilemmas and solutions, the stronger they emerge. At this juncture it can be asked whether this emergent strength can continue to hold even if despair and self-deception are re-entered as future possibilities.

Self-deception and despair

Imelda: If all was going badly, how much do you think it would take for you to retract your statement?

Anne: To say that I didn't do it?

Imelda: Yeah.

Anne: Yeah . . . em . . . I don't think I could retract it now, eh . . . actually, I thought of that myself, you know, just saying, 'forget about it I didn't do it, it was all a ploy'. No, I don't think I could retract it.

Imelda: So you don't think that even Patrick might be able to persuade you to do that.

Anne: No, I don't think so.

Patrick: I wouldn't attempt to.

Imelda: You wouldn't attempt to.

Anne: No, it would have been all a waste then.

Patrick: It would only put the dilemma off for another three or four years.

Anne: It would have been all a complete waste, me after facing up to what I did, for me to turn around and say, 'all right I didn't do it', I think it would be total . . . after all I went through in the past four or five months and that I put everyone else through, not only Patrick but my family too. No, it would mean then that was a total waste.

Anne has been tempted to retract her disclosure, 'actually I thought of that myself'. However, a commitment to the truth for the event and for all that they have suffered since is juxtaposed with self-deception as a wasted life, a marker for despair. In giving this its full significance the possibility for a more comprehensive meaning is secured.

A place of shared understanding and responsibility: a Fifth Province is co-created

Anne: Em ... well, I suppose if the worst came to the worst and it was really that bad I probably would, yeah, because it was all my fault in the first place.

Patrick: No it wasn't.

Anne: Most of it was.

Patrick: No. *(Shakes his head)*

Anne: I mean if I had been more honest with Patrick and turned round and said, 'I can't cope, I can't do this' instead of thinking that I could do everything and then, I actually did do it, you know. Yeah, I would be more prepared if I felt that it would mean that Michael was safe and at home with his family.

Imelda: OK in terms of Patrick's blindness. How sighted is he now at the moment?

Anne (smiles and laughs): Well, he is better, we are getting there slowly.

Imelda: How is he showing that to you? How are you seeing he is less blind to you?

Anne: Because I think that he is listening more, he is not just being fobbed off [conned] liked previously. I could just fob him off and say, 'Everything is OK. I am doing this, that and the other' you know. He would just take my word for what it was. I think more he is listening to what I am saying and as regards the bills, I show him I pay so he knows exactly where he stands on that. He sits down more and he talks better. Like before, if we were talking he would have one ear on the TV and one ear on what I was saying *(laughs)* whereas I think now he listens to what I say and he doesn't take things at face value that everything is all right. He doesn't just leave it at that. He is more prepared to persevere and say, 'are you sure?' and 'what is this?'

Patrick contextualizes the event by acknowledging the part he has played. Anne does not diminish her part, 'I actually did do it, you know'. Patrick's positioning in the unfolding events has been to persevere and in this way he has retained hope. It is this term that Anne uses to describe his renewed efforts to listen to her and perhaps to understand her. 'He is more prepared to persevere and say, "are you sure?".' They have come into their own ground and reached the 'first circle of themselves' again (Hederman 1985: 113).

Conclusion

Throughout this interview we have presented hope and despair in dialectical interplay. Anne and Patrick, as parents under state surveillance, persevered with us in a dialectical enquiry that brought forth a redeemed future from events of failure. Through an 'as if' dis-positioning at the extremes of this dialectic, a space was co-created with them and witnessed by their professional helpers in which the realities of child protection and family integrity were constantly juxtaposed. Questions at the extreme were employed in the opening out of what was already implicitly known. These questions presupposed a trust in the dialectical mediation of contradictions, in this case hope and despair, to produce conversational realities and relationship forms unforeseen at the outset.

As the interview progressed, the couple courageously encountered the possibilities of an extreme past (filicide) and future (family dispersal). At each extreme a new facet of emergent responsibility was glimpsed. Old failures were faced and in each facing stronger parents emerged.

Hope and despair are the immanent companions of what is tragic and free in the human condition, a transcendence overcoming what is fated and determined. The juxtaposition of hope and despair resonates with situations of crisis or catastrophe common in our understanding and yet not amenable to objective consideration. It may be a manner of reflection of some individual experience, one's own or some other, or a collective response in a shared event. It speaks to a bleak situation where more is called for than contrasting cognitive–affective appraisals of optimism or pessimism adequate for action–inaction in problem-solving. The latter fits within an established horizon of expectation and meaning and where favourable or unfavourable outcomes reflect human effort, good or bad fortune. Outside or beyond this orientation to the future, to expectancy, hope and despair is a moral meditation on the question of whether life is worth living and is a manifestation of human freedom: 'this spiritual freedom which cannot be taken away that makes life meaningful and purposeful' (Frankl 1962: 66).

This moral meditation on hope and despair by Patrick and Anne is an acknowledgement of their failures, of what they have endured and what they can hope for. With these hopes a new social relationship emerged that conferred meaningfulness and connection on their previously unwanted child. On the ground of shared understanding and responsibility the way forward for Michael to come home was forged.

Notes

1　A Fifth Province dialectic is one in which there is a co-creation with conversational partners of a 'reality' which allows clients and therapists to 'go on' in situations of apparent contradiction.
2　Writing in this vein about the Fifth Province in 1985, Hederman reaffirms that the notion of a fifth province does not have a fixed physical or geographical location. Rather it is a 'place beyond or behind the reach of our normal scientific consciousness'. As he sees it, it is also a centre or space beyond the psychology of the single individual (the ego) – a space which gives access to the transcendent (Hederman 1985: 111).

References

Anderson, P. (1992) *A Zone of Engagement*. London: Verso.

Barash, M. (1999) Despair in the medieval imagination, *Hope and Despair, A Special Issue, Social Research*, 66(2): 529–50.

Bloch, E. (1986) *The Principle of Hope*. London: Basil Blackwell.

Camus, A. (1968) *Lyrical and Critical Essays*, ed. Philip Thody, trans. Ellen Conroy Kennedy. New York: Vintage Books.

Colgan, F.I. (1991) The Fifth Province Model: father–daughter incest disclosure and systemic consultation, PhD dissertation, University College Dublin.

Frankl, V. (1962) *Man's Search for Meaning*, Boston, MA: Beacon Press.

Fukuyama, J. (1992) *The End of History and the Last Man*. London: Penguin.

Hederman, M.P. (1985) Poetry and the Fifth Province, *The Crane Bag*, 9: 110–19.

Kant, I. (1961) *Critique of Pure Reason*. London: Macmillan.

Lasch, C. (1991) *The True and Only Heaven*. New York: W.W. Norton.

Marcel, G. (1995) *The Philosophy of Existentialism*, trans. Manya Harari. New York: Carol Publishing Group.

Marcel, G. (1951) *Homo Viator: Introduction to Metaphysics of Hope*. London: Victor Gollancz.

Milosz, Czeslaw (2001) *The Captive Mind*, trans. Jane Zienonko. London: Penguin Classics.

Rorty, R. (1998) *Achieving Our Country*. Cambridge, MA: Harvard University Press.

Part 2

Facing adversity: practices of hope

Chapter 4

Hope: the far side of despair

Monica McGoldrick and Paulette Moore Hines

> I do not understand human existence ... apart from hope and dream ...
> And hopelessness is but hope that has lost its bearings.
>
> (Freire 1994: 8)

The importance of hope

Hope is a concept central to all therapy, as it is to all life, and hope is an action verb. As Paolo Freire (1994) made so clear, hope requires action to grow and transform our lives. Working with our clients around issues of hope is part of our clinical work every day. At the same time it is not something we can give to our clients. So what is it we can do in relation to hope? At some level, the effort to connect clients with wellsprings of hope is like Zen practice. It is not something that can be taught directly. Hope is at its core a spiritual belief in belonging to something larger than ourselves, a belief that whatever trauma we experience at present or carry forward from the past can be transformed into possibilities for the future. Somehow our clinical job in relation to hope is to help clients connect with their own spiritual resources, their own sources of hope. That is, we help them access their own belief in resources that can keep them going when they feel despair. But how do we do this? We do this by reminding our clients that they are a part of something larger than themselves and helping them to see themselves in context. Indeed, people belong in many contexts: time, space, the life cycle, family, community and social forces, nature and spiritual forces, gender, culture, class, racial hierarchies and constructs. So, let us first put ourselves and our perspective in some context.

I (MM) am a white, privileged, heterosexual social worker-therapist of Irish heritage, living and practicing in the US. I am also a 'woman of a certain age', the oldest generation now alive in my family, married over 35 years, mother of one son and godmother to many more young adults. The context in which my experience has taken place is one in which I have had many advantages educationally, professionally and socially. So the hopelessness that so many of my countrymen have experienced because of poverty, racism, classism, anti-Semitism or heterosexism are all experiences I have been spared. I have not been spared the pain of sexism and personal loss, but in general my privileges have surely limited my awareness of the experience of hopelessness in many ways.

I (PMH) am an African American, heterosexual clinical/community psychologist and family therapist, living and practicing in the US. I grew up in a working-class family, embedded in a large extended family context. I have been married for over 30 years, am the mother of two adult sons, an active part of the notion that it takes a village to raise a child (i.e. second mother to my niece's children), godmother to four young adults, daughter to parents who are still alive and niece to many second mothers (aunts), who, like my parents, are experiencing the challenges of ageing. I experienced the segregated South and grew up during the Civil Rights Movement in the US. The multiple oppressions of racism and sexism have been an ongoing part of my life; though I have never struggled with poverty, it too is intimately familiar. I have experienced the privilege that education affords and have directly witnessed the triple jeopardy encountered by family and acquaintances because of poverty, racism, and sexism.

This chapter will focus on the dilemmas of US therapists working with clients who have been exposed through their history to traumatic injuries at a personal, family, and cultural level. Clients' clinical presentations are often compounded by feelings of anger, rage, and hopelessness. Thus, fostering hope can be complicated, not only because clients may be subject to one multi-layered, traumatizing experience after another, but also because of therapists' well-intended but often misguided actions. In a nation in which the idea of a 'just society' is a vision that we have never really embraced, effective intervention requires us as therapists to assess our own social positions of power and privilege and their implications for our work with clients whose everyday lives are colored by inequities in every imaginable way. Many political, historical, and economic factors engender feelings, beliefs, and coping strategies that can complicate the healing of clients who face complex, overwhelming, and frequently unrelenting oppression. Therapists may unwittingly add further insult to clients' injuries by not recognizing or 'naming' trauma related to racism, sexism, heterosexism, and classism. Failing to acknowledge multigenerational cultural, societal, and familial trauma leaves clients mystified and isolated. It is our job to promote clients' hope, resilience, and healing by fostering their sense of connection and belonging. Although we can abuse our influence, the fact is we convey messages through our omissions as well as through what we say and do in therapy. As Ogden Nash (1962) in another context says, 'if it be some kind of sin we must be pursuing, better it be sins of commission than sins of omission' (p. 67). Our silence about multigenerational trauma when clients have internalized the pain of multiple levels of oppression can suck away their chances for hope, by leaving them cut off from the contextualization that would provide them with hope.

We can only help clients to free themselves from fears and pathological thinking which leads them to feel overwhelmed by the 'stuckness', darkness, or pain of their experiences, by helping them see themselves in context. This freedom becomes the light of possibilities for transformation. A mother may have lost her only child; nothing will make her a mother again as she was before; but she can realize there are other children to love, if she can expand her concept of belonging to include godchildren, nieces, nephews, and the children of her friends.

Hope is not a Pollyanna attitude of optimism. As Cornel West puts it: 'One can never understand what hope is really about unless one wrestles with despair' (1999: 554). According to Greek mythology, Pandora's box contained all the ills of the world and only one blessing: hope. What a burden for that one virtue! The mission of hope was to heal the wounds inflicted by all the other ills of life. Hope was the one salve the gods gave to deal with all the other ills of the world. This story conveys the crucial importance of hope for human survival. In his book *Hope Dies Last* (2003), Studs Terkel quotes a farm worker, Jessie de la Cruz, who said of the farm workers' efforts before Cesar Chavez united them: 'I feel there's gonna be a change, but we're the ones gonna do it, not the government. With us, there's a saying, "*La esperanza muere ultima*. Hope dies last". You can't lose hope. If you lose hope, you lose everything' (p. xv). That attitude reflects two crucial aspects of hope – its role as our last recourse and its ability to transform our future by mobilizing us for action. These two dimensions are what make hope such an important concept for psychotherapy:

- the ability of hope to help us envision a future; and
- the importance of our becoming the authors of our own lives.

To paraphrase bell hooks: when you speak or write in your own voice, you become subject rather than object – you transform your own destiny (hooks 1989). Thus, hope is an emotional and spiritual verb, but it is also an action verb, and all of those dimensions are important in therapy. It is our role as therapists to help clients find the resources within themselves and with each other to transform their pain into hope for changing their future. A profoundly touching example of this active transformative role of hope is the statement of a mother to the teenager who had murdered her own teenage son: 'You came into my life through an act of violence, but I see you now as part of my family. So, as part of the family you have a responsibility to hold this family in prayer – to do what you can to help us recover, because you've torn the family apart' (Oldershaw and Oldershaw 2003: 7). The mother in this powerful imperative puts forth her own hope and challenges the young man to share her hope and to join in transforming his own and their lives from the dreadful act of killing her son. Thus hope is always interpersonal. It is always about being in it together.

Therapists' training and limited personal experience often make it difficult to think outside the box as is necessary in such clinical situations. It helps to have a framework which can help us to be effective change agents. As therapists we need a framework which can help us understand our own as well as our clients' place in the wider social context from which to foster hope in our clients to deal with their multigenerational traumas.

Instilling hope in therapy

(Case of MM) Marion Irwin sought help because, she said, her close Jewish family was being torn apart. Her 32-year-old niece, Sarah, had revealed that, from as early as she could remember, she had been sexually abused by her grandfather, the beloved family patriarch, who had now been dead for 15 years. Marion said that this niece was viewed as 'impossible' – histrionic, demanding, critical, moody, and generally unpleasant since childhood. The main issue was that Sarah was now blaming everyone in the family for letting this abuse go on – her parents and her grandmother, whom she had cut off after bringing her into one angry family therapy session. The family, who were always very close, were now being forced to take sides and Marion's own daughters were angry with her for not being more supportive of their cousin. For many years the grandparents, who were close to both of their daughters, Marion and Ruth, had divided their time between New Jersey where Marion and her family lived and Florida where Ruth and her husband lived with their daughter, Sarah. Marion was angry with her niece, but also with her mother, feeling that her own daughters' criticism of her was a result of problems that were not her fault.

Upon close questioning, Marion admitted that her father had once fondled her as well. Years ago she had mentioned this fact to a therapist who had said, 'Didn't you realize you had been abused?' She dropped out of the therapy, assuming the therapist was making much out of nothing, since it had happened only once. The grandmother, Joan Stein, now 82, was fearful she would have a heart attack over these issues and wanted it all to go away. Marion was reluctant to bring her mother into the therapy, but realized that the family was in such turmoil that something had to be done.

The grandmother felt beleaguered by everyone and said she often thought of suicide. She had been married 'happily' for 45 years to her high-school sweetheart and now at age 82 she was being forced to justify her whole life over and over again to the other family members.

When pressed about details, she did remember coming in on her husband fondling Marion when she was a young teenager and had told him to 'cut it out'. She also remembered that her husband had once lost his job as a carpet cleaner because of accusations about his 'inappropriate' behavior with females. There had also been accusations made against her husband years before by a neighbor, who accused him of sexually abusing her little daughter. At that point Joan had insisted they see a psychiatrist, who saw her once and told her she should not get 'overwrought' by the situation. He proceeded to see the husband alone for several years until at some point the husband said he didn't need therapy any more. No further questions were ever asked.

Now, a generation later, Sarah was saying that the beloved grandfather, Bert, had sexually abused her for years. He had even fondled her in the swimming pool while all the family were actually present. Over the weeks and months that the history began to unfold, Marion, Ruth and the other granddaughters asked their friends if they had ever been uncomfortable around the grandfather. There were numerous reports of his inappropriate touching of family friends. Sarah had been left alone with him almost daily throughout her childhood, because he was retired and the others were working. The following descriptions of the therapy will be in the first person to maintain a personal connection to the work.

Helping to engender hope

I (MM) sought a way to open up for the grandmother a sense of hope through the value of her love for her family that would strengthen her for the family tasks required of her on behalf of her children and grandchildren. I was deeply touched by this family at the same time that I felt almost physically ill about what the grandfather had done to his granddaughter and to so many others in the family. I was touched also by Marion's courage in seeking help for herself, her mother, and her children. I was touched also by Marion's husband, Henry, who somehow managed to maintain a loving and supportive attitude toward all the family, while encouraging them to struggle through their feelings. And I was touched by the grandmother's willingness to confront the pain of the situation, even though she was facing such dreadful memories of her own silence and failure to act, and such horrific realities about a man she had loved for over 60 years.

As therapist, I thought it pivotal to help her face up to her granddaughter's accusation, and to those of her daughters and other grandchildren, for not having acknowledged the signs that were there of her husband's traumatizing and destructive behavior. Joan found it almost unbearable to focus on these issues, saying repeatedly that she felt she had been victimized as well. She was gradually realizing that her own father had abused her throughout her childhood, coming into her bed and holding her inappropriately close to his private parts. Her sense of victimization left her feeling isolated and helpless. She was ashamed to tell her friends, which made her feel even more alone. She said she cried all day and wanted to give up on life. She could not find any reason to hope in her life. Her once close, loving family had now been destroyed and she felt she was being blamed for it.

Hope begins on the far side of despair

Paolo Freire believed that without rage and love there can be no hope. He once said that in seeking the deepest 'why' of our pain, we are educating our hope (1994). I think that in our work with clients we are following Freire's concept. He was very specific about the active quality of hope in relation to his own depression as a young man:

I began to take my depression as an object of curiosity and investigation. I 'stepped back' from it, to learn its 'why.' Basically, I needed to shed some light on the framework in which it was being generated. At bottom, in seeking for the deepest 'why' of my pain, I was educating my hope ... I worked on things, on facts, on my will. I invented the concrete hope in which, one day I would see myself delivered from my depression.

(1994: 28–9)

This is the work we try to do in therapy – help people explore their experience in ways which link their past, present, and potential future, creating hope for transformation. As Freire (1994: 8–9) says, hope alone does not win. The naive idea that hope alone will transform the world is an excellent route to hopelessness, pessimism, and fatalism. There is no hope in sheer hopefulness. The hoped-for is not attained by dint of raw hoping. Hope does not have the power to transform reality all by itself. No. Hope is necessary, but not enough. It needs an anchoring practice in action in order to become historical concreteness.

For Joan it was only when she could see her own immortality in her children and grandchildren, or in the future history of women, who will rise up and not be silent about sexual objectification and abuse of girls, that she could find a sense of hopefulness to imagine that suicide was not the answer to her pain. She had to go beyond the pain of having to rewrite her history including the disillusionment, trauma, despair, and heartbreak so she could begin to free herself to be the creator of a new liberating chapter in her family, her culture, and human history's story of the treatment of girls and women.

I (MM) tried to help her recognize that she was a pioneer, who, by her courage in facing these excruciatingly painful realities, could be a mentor for all the women of future generations of her family. We spoke about who had been a mentor to her in her life, about the mentoring she had wished she had from her own mother when her father molested her, her mentoring of her daughters which had made them strong enough to be courageously struggling now to change things for the whole family. We spoke about the Jews who survived the Holocaust and dared, through their gestures large and small, to create a space of hope for future generations of Jews.

Her daughter Ruth came for one session in which she expressed great sympathy for her mother, but gave her the wise advice that whenever Joan was inclined to feel angry at Sarah she should imagine Sarah as being not 32, but 5, the age she was when she was first sexually abused by her grandfather. Ruth thought this might help her mother recognize her power as an adult to support the next generation. We discussed Joan's own sources of strength in those who had come before that had loved her. She was encouraged to think about what messages she wanted to leave for her grandchildren to pass on to their children about how to handle painful experiences in life.

Connecting with the past in order to connect in the present and have possibilities for the future

The question is how to 'keep hope alive.' How do people keep their spirits intact even though they have been repeatedly traumatized, dehumanized or made to feel invisible or powerless? For many people who have experienced generations of oppression, just to survive with a belief in themselves and the ability to love others is a major tribute to hope.

In the movie *Amistad* (1997), Cinque, the Mende African leader of a slave revolt, tells John Quincy Adams that he will not be going to court alone. Adams replies, no, because we have righteousness on our side. Cinque responds that he will not be alone for another reason: 'I meant my ancestors. I will call into the past, far back to the beginning of time, and beg them to come and help me ... I will reach back and draw them into me. And they must come. For at this moment I am the whole reason they have existed at all.'

When people encounter a situation where there appears no hope at all, they can invoke their ancestors. If one can summon the spirit of one's ancestors, then they have never left. And the wisdom and strength they inspired will come to our aid. This concept that we are always part of what has gone before and what will be in the future seems to be essential to hope.

Susan, a 35 year-old lesbian Episcopalian minister, grew up as the only child of Southern Baptist parents. She had made great efforts to work out a relationship with her very judgmental mother, to the point that she had decided to give a sermon in her mother's church, which had been her family's parish for many generations. As Susan prepared for her sermon she became extremely anxious about their condemnation of her for her 'sin' of being lesbian. Sitting in the front of the church waiting for the service to begin she struggled to find a source of hope and suddenly she had a fantasy of her grandmother, great-grandmothers and great-aunts sitting in the front row supporting her. This sense of the presence of her strong female ancestors came to her intuitively, not because she tried to call them forth, but perhaps because she was letting herself experience her fear and grow beyond it. Her sense that they were there for her somehow gave her hope and courage to pro-ceed and she spoke confidently in a sermon many parishioners found deeply moving.

Susan still struggles to hold on to her hope for transformation within Christian communities, so many of which continue to denigrate homo-sexuality. She draws strength and hope in her work and her personal efforts from her ancestors, who, even though they themselves would undoubtedly have been homophobic, nevertheless had the strength to challenge many social inequities in their own lives. Susan connects with them when she struggles to help her mother achieve the confidence to contend with her own network – her friends' and relatives' homo-phobia. Susan's hope comes not only from the family connectedness she anticipates she and her partner will be able to have with her mother in the years to come, but also from her belief in the importance of the changes she is trying to bring about for those lesbians, gays, and trans-sexuals in the next generations who may experience less hatred and prejudice in part because of her efforts. Perhaps symbolically they were also there in that congregation that day with her ancestors.

In other situations lancing the wounds of the past in order to achieve freedom for the future requires more painful retracing of our steps. Tom Mathews (2005a), author of *Our Fathers' War*, has described the pivotal moment in his relationship with his father, who had returned from World War II remote, moody, demanding, and a heavy drinker. Tom's relationship with his father had been shut down since the day his father returned from the war and called him, at age 3, a coward for not jumping down from a roof. Having been cut off from his father for several years, he finally decided, when his father turned 80, to invite him to revisit the path he had taken in the war. His father agreed to the journey. At first it just seemed like a father–son outing, but then, one day, as they talked in a café, the father suddenly gave a strangled sob: 'I killed a lot of people. Jesus Christ, I killed so many people!' adding a few minutes later, 'I've never said that to anyone. I've never said that even to myself' (Mathews 2005a: 268–9).

Somehow, in that moment of daring to connect with the dreadful truth of his history and in daring to speak of it, he created hope for both himself and his son. Shut-down is about loss of hope, connection is about hope – hope that, no matter what has happened, no matter what we have done or what has been done to us, there are possibilities of transformation. Later that evening the father reflected that he thought he was coming to understand what was happening: 'All that youth, all that spirit, all that courage and then what you see is that you've turned into a killing machine. You look and see something you have in yourself, something atavistic' (Mathews 2005a: 269). After that evening, Tom says: 'The code was cracked. After that we were able to talk, and it transformed our lives' (Mathews 2005b: 4). It seems as if the father's final daring to face the horror of what he did freed him to connect with himself and with his son.

A lot of effort had gone into Tom's invitation to take his father to the place of his war trauma. He had begun to think that his father's experience was a cultural experience – one that connected all those who shared the killing in the war. He was ready for his father's truth, which perhaps supported his father in telling it. This is the role we as therapists can play, to support our clients moving through the despair of their lives. We must be ready to receive it if we are going to help them move past it. We must be able to tolerate the horror, and we must be ready to believe them.

Dilemmas for white therapists in dealing with clients of color

In order to support our clients' efforts to find hope through the 'why' of their pain, we must also consider the structures of privilege and oppression that shape our experiences of hope and pain in this society, and how our own social location may make it more difficult for us to empathize with the experience of others.

There is always particular difficulty for those in positions of privilege to understand the experience of the oppressed. For example, for white people in the US, their distance from experiences of racism over many generations makes it hard to identify with or even hear the experiences of trauma caused by multiple generations of prejudice, subjugation, and trauma of clients of color. Perhaps the hardest part of responding clinically to clients of color if you are white is the difficulty of staying conscious of what the wounds of racism do to a person, since these micro-aggressions have never been focused on us. Whites live life, as Peggy McIntosh (1998) has put it, with a knapsack of free checks and credit cards, which permit going through life and never experiencing anything but positive responses to the color of their skin. As the saying goes, it is as if whites were born on third base and we always think that we hit a home run. The experience of our whiteness always giving us messages that we are 'OK' leads us to misjudge the effort for a person who never gets those 'OK' messages. White therapists must be vigilant in listening, because we have been so shaped by our own experiences not to hear and not to believe that these experiences could be so real and so pervasive. And we must let ourselves be shocked every time. The practice of becoming aware and staying aware of racism takes some doing.

For clients of color, it is very hard to forget what has happened, while for white therapists it is very hard to remember. Thus, when white therapists are in the position of helping clients of color find sources of hope they may have particular difficulty. Beyond careful listening, therapists must believe clients and take a position of acknowledgment and validation, before we can win their trust to help them explore possible sources of hope. Hope begins on the far side of despair, so therapists must acknowledge clients' pain in order to support their moving beyond it to hope. Our acknowledgment of the experiences that have oppressed and mystified our clients helps them get their footing, after which they can connect with the beliefs that become their sources of hope. Perhaps the greatest training white therapists could make for this process of listening and acknowledgment is to think what their own privilege, or lack of it, may have done to them. How has it hardened their hearts or made them believe they actually deserve the special treatment they get more than people of color do? Therapy with clients of color requires that therapists be continuously vigilant about our own perceptual limitations, even as we try to help clients find sources of hope in a context, which continuously undermines them.

Beliefs, spirituality, religion, and hope

There is a clear relationship between our beliefs and our emotional and behavioral functioning. Beliefs may either serve as anchors during the storm of a crisis to maintain and encourage hope and resilience or promote a sense of hopelessness and helplessness (Walsh 1998).

The training of most therapists does not encourage us to deal with spiritual beliefs and values (Hines 1998; Walsh 1999). The anxiety associated with addressing religious beliefs is even greater, for a variety of reasons. Discussing religion, like money or death, has become a taboo for many therapists. Perhaps this is because of the belief that therapists are supposed to maintain 'neutrality'; therefore, discussing religion will go too directly into issues of prescribed values. Or it may be because of the ways that religion has been misused to support oppression. But in our view, discussing spiritual and religious beliefs is extremely important for helping clients to explore their own values and especially to think out of the box in order to connect with potential sources of hope.

The following are some questions we have found helpful in exploring the connections between beliefs and hope:

- What were the beliefs you were taught when you were growing up that were meant to give you hope? What is your relationship to those beliefs now?
- What were the messages of hope that enabled people of your culture to survive, to live beyond failure or pain?
- What have been your greatest disillusionments in life and how did you move past them?
- Who loved you in your life? What messages did they give you about hope?
- What kept your mother going when she lost hope (also your father, grandmother, etc.)?
- What messages about hope do you want to leave for your grandchildren and others who will come after us?
- Is there someone you especially admire in terms of overcoming adversity and conveying a hopeful perspective?
- What would you wish people would say about you in your obituary? (Conversations about death are particularly useful in helping people connect with sources of hope beyond themselves – see McGoldrick 2004.)

In the face of such circumstances, for which there may be no concrete resolution, encouraging hope means motivating clients to make behavioral, spiritual, and cognitive shifts that can enhance their functioning and improve the quality of their lives, even where there are circumstances they cannot change (physical deterioration, financial, emotional, physical or spiritual distress, imminent death or the loss of a loved one). Hopelessness is a loss of will, a will that is necessary to pursue possibilities, however limited these may be. We can nourish our own hope and that of our clients by attending to our connection to our ancestors and to our descendants, tapping into our cultural legacies – those we inherit and those we will leave behind.

References

Freire, P. (1994) *The Pedagogy of Hope*. New York: Continuum.
hooks, b. (1989) *Talking Back*. Cambridge, MA: South End Press.
McGoldrick, M. (2004) Legacies of loss, in F. Walsh and M. McGoldrick (eds) *Living Beyond Loss*, 2nd edn. New York: Norton.

McIntosh, P. (1998) Unpacking the invisible knapsack of privilege, in M. McGoldrick (ed.) *Revisioning Family Therapy: Race, Culture and Gender in Clinical Practice*. New York: Guilford.

Mathews, T. (2005a) *Our Fathers' War*. New York: Broadway Books.

Mathews, T. (2005b) Interview with Terence Smith, PBS, *The News Hour*, 10 August.

Nash, O. (1962) *The Pocketbook of Ogden Nash*. New York: Pocket Books.

Oldershaw, R. and Oldershaw, J. (2003) Brothers, in S. Terkel (ed.) *Hope Dies Last: Keeping the Faith in Difficult Times*. New York: The New Press.

Terkel, S. (ed.) (2003) *Hope Dies Last: Keeping the Faith in Difficult Times*. New York: The New Press.

Walsh, F. (1998) *Strengthening Family Resilience*. New York: Guilford.

Walsh, F. (ed.) (1999) *Spiritual Resources in Family Therapy*. New York: Guilford.

West, C. (1999) *The Cornel West Reader*. Boston, MA: Beacon Press.

Chapter 5

Despair, resistance, hope: response-based therapy with victims of violence

Allan Wade

Introduction

Eric Blair (George Orwell) (Orwell 1937) made several trips to visit coal mining families in northern England in preparation for *The Road to Wigan Pier*. From his seat on the train ride home after one of those trips he observed a young woman in her back yard, trying to free a clogged drainpipe:

> She had a round pale face, the usual exhausted face of the slum girl who is twenty-five and looks forty, thanks to miscarriages and drudgery; and it wore ... the most desolate, hopeless expression I have ever seen. It struck me then that we are mistaken when we say that 'It isn't the same for them as it would be for us', and that people bred in the slums can imagine nothing but the slums. For what I saw in her face was not the ignorant suffering of an animal. She knew well enough what was happening to her – understood as well as I did how dreadful a destiny it was to be kneeling there in the bitter cold, on the slimy stones of a slum backyard, poking a stick up a foul drain-pipe.
>
> (Orwell 1937: 15)

This passage marks an important shift in Orwell's perspective on themes that recur throughout his essays and political fiction – how oppression works on the individual and how the individual responds. It also points to a distinction between contrasting views of 'the oppressed': a determinist or 'effects-based' view in which oppression is presumed to condition the mind of the individual to the point that she acts as an accomplice in the oppression she endures, and a 'response-based' view in which the individual responds to and resists subjugation, overtly and covertly, through myriad psychological and social tactics woven into the fabric of daily life. It is the latter view applied to the practice of therapy that I describe briefly in this chapter, primarily through two case examples.

Orwell (1937: 15) sees that the 'desolate, hopeless expression' of the slum girl points not to 'ignorant suffering', which is commonly imputed to individuals who face poverty or oppression, but to its polar opposite, her direct comprehension of the conditions that oppress her. The despair she conveys cannot be construed accurately as an *effect* or *impact of* those conditions but must be viewed as a *directional response* that signals her *orientation to* those conditions *as adverse*. Struck by this realization, Orwell puts the lie to two myths that provide the middle and upper classes with a sense of invulnerability and prop up the smug condescension with which they regard the oppressed – that 'it isn't the same for them as it would be for us' and that 'people bred in the slums can imagine nothing but the slums'.

Interpreted more broadly, the passage reflects Orwell's concern with questions that preoccupied him from the age of 8, when the headmistress of St Cyprian's school publicly humiliated him for wetting his bed, until his death just after completing *Nineteen Eighty-Four* (1949) and 'Such, Such Were the Joys' (1952), the sardonically titled essay about his school experiences that he found so painful to write (Shelden 1991). Faced with isolation, surveillance, strict regulation and vicious retribution for any form of self-assertion or dissent, how does an individual build up a psychological barrier between himself and his tormentors behind which he can manufacture some sense of safety, autonomy and self-worth? When open defiance is too dangerous, how do victims express their indignation and act upon their desire for justice? What strategies do the architects of repression use to establish secrecy, enforce conformity and eliminate dissent? More specifically, how do they use language to represent their actions as beneficial and just?

Resistances as acts of hope in the face of desperate times

Orwell (1946: 187) addressed these questions not on the level of ideological debate, which too easily descends into a contest of abstractions, but through the 'window pane' of lucid prose. He spoke convincingly to his contemporaries living under Stalin because he exposed in fine detail both the mechanics of totalitarianism where it meets the individual and the individual's overt and covert responses. When open defiance is impractical or too dangerous, resistance is expressed indirectly and on the micro-level of social interaction. For Jewish prisoners in Nazi concentration camps resistance consisted in part of living in accordance with the 'ordinary virtues': the maintenance of dignity, care for others, respect for moral standards and the love of aesthetic pleasure (Todorov 1990). For Aboriginal children who were imprisoned and subjected to physical, sexualized and psychological torture in residential schools, resistance consisted in part of protecting one another, escaping the terror of abuse by mentally leaving the scene, stealing food, retaining connections with family and culture and contesting the authority of their abusers whenever possible (Fournier and Crey 1997).

Milosz ([1951] 1990: 54) observed that, under Stalin, ordinary relationships took on the form of acting:

Such acting is a highly developed craft that places a premium upon mental alertness. Before it leaves the lips, every word must be evaluated as to its consequences. A smile that appears at the wrong moment, a glance that is not all it should be can occasion dangerous suspicions and accusations. Even one's gestures, tone of voice, or preference for certain kinds of neckties are interpreted as signs of one's political tendencies.

The alertness to situational detail that effective acting requires can be exhausting, but if relaxed can result in exposure and disastrous consequences. To obtain a 'sense of relief' from this constant vigilance and to ensure that 'the proper reflexes at the proper moment become truly automatic', the individual may find it necessary to 'identify . . . with the role [he] is obliged to play' (Milosz [1951] 1990: 55).

But acting has its limits. Self-respect and dignity depend in part on the individual's ability to maintain 'coherence between internal standards and external behaviour' (Todorov 1990: 69). In some circumstances the gap between what is psychologically true for the individual and what he is able to practise outwardly can grow to massive proportions. Resistance may then take the form of eccentric or apparently self-destructive behaviour. Nerzin, one of the political prisoners in Solzhenitsyn's novel *The First Circle* (1968), rejected his comparatively privileged status and refused a job that would have led to his early release because, he asserted, 'a healthy plebeian attitude is . . . the only worthy basis for a relation to human beings and their community' (Lukacs 1969: 62–3).

Some Jewish prisoners in Nazi concentration camps committed suicide as a final act of self-determination, to deny the Nazis the absolute control they desired (Todorov 1990). Others sang songs on their way to the gas chamber or entered prior to their appointed time to accompany loved ones. Knowing that they would be brutally beaten, many Aboriginal children challenged the authority of the school supervisors. One woman reported that at age 8 she was strapped until her hands bled onto the floor and still refused to cry. She asserted, 'I would never give them that' (Wade 2000: 67). Gomes (2004: 31) described a young woman who for a period of time engaged in self-harm as a form of resistance to sexualized abuse. She remarked, 'If I had not been cutting, I probably would have died a long time ago.' To romanticize these acts would be to overlook the pain and desperation from which they arise. And yet to judge them self-destructive or merely eccentric would be to miss their meaning entirely: it is through these acts that we glimpse 'the inextinguishable inner activity of a humanity defending itself' (Lukacs 1969: 60).

Bell hooks (1990: 341) argued that it is important to locate resistance on the margins and *in* the experience of despair because marginalized people are widely represented as submissive by writers who would reduce their complex responses to a single, apolitical dimension – individual pain:

Understanding marginality as position and place of resistance is crucial for oppressed, exploited, colonized people. If we only view the margin as sign, marking the condition of our pain and deprivation, then a certain hopelessness and despair, a deep nihilism penetrates in a destructive way the very ground of our being. It is there in that space of collective despair that one's creativity, one's imagination is at risk, there that one's mind is fully colonized, there that the freedom one longs for is lost.

(hooks 1990: 342)

Despair both embodies and engenders resistance (Adams 2005) while it affirms the insatiable desire for freedom and dignity. What a person *despairs against* points to what she *hopes for* (Reynolds 2001).

Sociopolitical violence committed in the context of totalitarianism cannot be equated with personalized violence such as sexualized assault and abuse, wife-assault, physical assault, verbal abuse or workplace harassment: the structural differences between the two cases are simply too pronounced (Scott 1990). One essential similarity, however, is that both types of violence rely on misrepresentation. In personalized violence misrepresentation has less to do with *doublespeak*, an orchestrated campaign of propaganda complete with its own neologisms, prohibited terminology and odd grammar, than it does with *oldspeak*, the habitual use of obsolete terms, vague grammar and stale metaphors that (a) conceal violence, (b) mitigate perpetrators' responsibility, (c) conceal victims' responses and resistance and (d) blame or pathologize victims (Todd and Wade 2003; Coates and Wade 2004).

The linguistic devices that locally accomplish these discursive operations feature prominently in courtrooms, psychotherapy literature and journalism (Coates *et al.* 2000; Todd and Wade 2003; Coates and Wade 2004). Although violent acts are unilateral in nature, they are often represented as mutual or even erotic acts: rape is referred to as 'unwanted sex' and wife-assault as 'an argument' or a 'domestic dispute' (Coates 1996). Although violence is deliberate, as evinced by perpetrators' strategic efforts to suppress victims' resistance, it is widely represented as an effect of social, biological or psychological forces that overwhelm the perpetrator and compel him to perform violent acts (O'Neill and Morgan 2001; Coates and Wade 2004). Although victims invariably respond to and resist violence (Kelly 1988; hooks 1990; Scott 1990; Burstow 1992; Wade 1997, 2000), therapy is typically conceptualized as a process of treating effects or impacts. And while resistance is ubiquitous, victims are widely represented as perpetrators of their own misfortunes (e.g. Engel 1990; Herman 1997).

Language and ideology

Oldspeak is so deeply embedded as the stock discourse on violence that it does not require an ideological commitment from its users. Rather, failure to speak in its terms amounts to a kind of deviant behaviour that is easily dismissed as zealous or ideological. The ubiquity of *oldspeak* means that beyond the violence itself victims are confronted with accounts that radically distort the facts, including their own physical, emotional, mental and spiritual responses. Still, they may have little choice but to use that language if they want to be treated as credible and provided with the necessary institutional support. I recently worked for a woman who was assaulted by her husband and then labelled uncooperative by the police, who refused to return her phone calls. When the attending officer asked, 'So, how long have you been having marriage problems?' her offence was to reply, 'Why are you asking about my marriage? This isn't a marriage problem, it's an assault'. For perpetrators *oldspeak* provides a handy social resource, a common parlance with legal and human service professionals that already obscures their responsibility and limits their exposure to negative consequences.

The language of effects in the dimming of hopefilled accounts

Especially important is that victims' responses are widely represented as effects. The language of effects is a highly interpretive repertoire that conceals victims' responses and resistance and represents victims as submissive. Indeed, what transforms responses and resistance into problems, and problems into symptoms, is precisely their representation as effects. To address this problem, Linda Coates, Nick Todd and I have been working on a 'response-based' approach to therapeutic interviewing which has required the development of specific interviewing practices and the modification of practices developed in the brief, systemic, solution-focused, narrative and feminist approaches. We focus not on treating effects but on elucidating individuals' physical, emotional, mental and spiritual responses to specific acts of violence and other forms of oppression and adversity. Certain responses – often the very problem itself – become intelligible as forms of resistance that point to 'symptoms of chronic mental wellness'. The examples of James and Nan provide a brief illustration.

Case examples: engendering hope through response-based interviewing

James

James (32) was referred for therapy three months after a group of young men assaulted him outside his home. One man 'sucker punched' him (i.e. punched him in the head from the side without warning). Then they all kicked him repeatedly in the body and head while he lay unconscious on the ground. James's mother Rita (55) witnessed the assault and ran to the door, yelling that she had called the police. James was hospitalized with concussion, bruised ribs and numerous cuts and bruises. Three of the youths were arrested and charged with assault, while two remained at large.

James was sleeping poorly, waking with nightmares, experiencing 'lots of anxiety' and 'panic attacks', and occasionally missing work. He had been living like a 'shut-in' because he was not interested in seeing friends and felt 'afraid to go out at night'. He had become increasingly isolated, 'testy' and 'impatient'. This put a strain on his relationship with Sarah (30), his girlfriend of several years. James stressed that he loved Sarah 'very much' but could not expect her to wait for him to get his life together. He said, 'I just can't commit. She wants to get married and have a family. But I just can't. I don't know what it is. I'm just not sure I'm ready for that. Maybe you can help me figure that out.' I made a mental note of the notion that James 'could not commit' and planned to return to the subject later in the interview after gathering more information.

I then asked James a few questions about his family, to get a better sense of his circumstances. James said that he was very close to his mother and his brother Bill (28). His parents separated when he was 8, after which he rarely saw his father. James said he 'went through a lot' in his childhood and disclosed that at 8 and 9 he was periodically sexually abused by his uncle. I remarked that James had not mentioned this as his reason for coming to counselling. He replied, 'Aw, what the hell, I've got to deal with this some time.' I then asked him to tell me a bit more about the timing and nature of the abuse, in general terms.

As James began to describe the first assault (when his uncle trapped him on the couch and forced him to put his hand on his – the uncle's – genitals), I asked him a three-part question about how he had responded at the time: 'When he tried to trap you and force you to touch him, how did you respond? You know, what did you do?' The first part of this question refers to the specific interaction and the uncle's actions in particular. The second part (i.e. 'how did you respond?') presupposes that James did indeed respond immediately and shifts the focus to those responses as the key topic. (McGee 1999). The third part, a tag question (i.e. 'what did you do?'), clarifies the word 'responses' by asking James to describe his overt behaviour.

With some additional questions (e.g., How did you do that? Then what happened? What else did you do?), James detailed many responses that I felt were clearly intelligible as forms of resistance: he felt uncomfortable, moved to the end of the couch, tried to get up, squirmed and wiggled to get away, said 'what are you doing' and 'don't', pulled his hand back, felt disgusted, refused to move his hand as instructed and averted his eyes. I then asked James how he changed his relationship with his uncle after the first assault. James said that he avoided his uncle, threatened to tell his mum and complained bitterly when his mother suggested that his uncle baby-sit. I asked if the uncle had also abused Bill. To this James replied, 'No way. I never let that bastard near Bill. I think I would have fucking killed him.' James described a number of ways in which he protected his younger brother, during and after the abuse.

I then recast a number of the responses James had described as forms of resistance through a *connective* question: 'Well . . . you know . . . it's clear that you resisted the abuse from your uncle in many ways, right from the beginning, even though you couldn't make it stop. Have there been other times when you've had to resist in this kind of way, or protect others?' James thought about this for a moment and then described how he had protected his mother once, when a boyfriend assaulted her. He also talked about his relationship with his brother in their teens. He admitted that he used to beat his brother up, badly. He said, 'You know, I never thought of it before. But I think what I was trying to do was keep him in line. I know that sounds stupid, but he was into some really strange shit. And it drove mum nuts. She used to call my uncle over (the same uncle) to straighten Bill out. He [Bill] hated me for a long time.' He then talked about how he had since taken responsibility for mistreating Bill and enjoyed a strong, respectful relationship with him.

I then felt as though I had enough information to return to the topic of James' apparent 'inability to commit' to Sarah. I asked, 'James, this might sound like a strange question, but have you ever worried that, because you were sexually abused as a child, you would be likely to abuse others?' At this, James started crying quietly. He said, 'Well, yeah. Isn't that right?' I explained that this was a popular myth that was not supported by careful research, nor likely given the nature of his conduct. 'It's pretty clear that you have resisted violence of every kind since you were little. We can see that in the way you resisted your uncle's violence, in the way you protected your brother and then took responsibility for hurting him, and in the way you protected your mum from violence. We can also see that by the fact that you have refused to commit yourself to Sarah because you have been quietly terrified that you might abuse your future children.' James cried heavily as we sat for a few moments without speaking.

I went on, 'If you were really a risk to abuse children, you would be only too eager to marry Sarah and have children that you could then exploit. And you probably wouldn't be telling a perfect stranger about your plans, would you? You know, if you suspected that you might be a risk to abuse children and then went ahead and married Sarah anyway, and had children with her, that would be a very serious problem, would it not? I think you have shown extraordinary commitment to Sarah: you have put your commitment to not abusing anyone before your desire to make a life with her. Really, what more profound commitment could you make to Sarah?' James was surprised at this perspective, and greatly relieved. We talked about what differences he might notice as a result of being more closely in touch with his own history of resistance and, in particular, the nature of his commitment to Sarah.

Two weeks later James brought Sarah to our scheduled appointment and reported a number of positive changes. He was working steadily, getting out and visiting with friends, had no further anxiety or panic attacks and had testified effectively in court. He and Sarah had been talking about setting a wedding date. 'It's strange,' he said, 'I don't really feel angry about the whole thing. I just want them to get some help so they don't hurt anyone else.'

Nan

Nan (48) came in because she was 'losing it all the time' and 'feeling really depressed'. Nan's husband Bob (52) had secretly made some bad financial decisions. He blamed Nan for their losses and pressured her to make more money. This was part of a broader pattern of emotionally abusive behaviour. I asked Nan how she had responded to Bob's pressure and accusations. She replied, 'That's what I mean. I don't do anything. I'm just such a cling-on.' By 'cling-on', Nan meant that she just could not 'let go', that she was 'dependent' and held on to 'dysfunctional relationships'. She said she was repeating a pattern that had been laid down by the women in her family.

I asked Nan to give me an example of being a 'cling-on'. She described how she had been physically assaulted by her first male partner, Chuck. One night Chuck became aggressive and punched Nan several times on the head and torso. Nan protected herself, yelled at him to stop, tried to keep him away with her feet, and finally found cover under their bed. Chuck gave up and fell asleep on the couch in the next room. Nan eventually crept out from under the bed, saw Chuck on the couch and went to sleep. The next morning Chuck was gone and had taken all his clothes. Nan could not find him but soon learned that he had returned to Amsterdam, his home town. Nan boarded the next available flight. 'Can you believe it,' she said incredulously, 'I followed him! How stupid can you be? I might as well wear a "hit me please" sign on my forehead.' I noted Nan's resistance to the assault but this did little to address her assertion that she was a 'cling-on'. Even if she resisted the assault, she still followed Chuck to Amsterdam.

It seemed to me that the phrase 'cling-on' encapsulated an effects-based interpretation of Nan's conduct, according to which Nan was conditioned to accept abuse and cling to abusive men. Moreover, this view was supported by a previous therapist and confirmed what her husband Bob had been saying for some time, that she was 'messed up' and needed to get her 'head on straight'. Although Nan had resisted Chuck's and Bob's abusive behaviour, she seemed to doubt her own instincts and ability to parent Tom (13). I felt that the label 'cling-on' distorted Nan's prudent responses and resistance to various forms of abuse and adversity. However, I could not immediately grasp how being a 'cling-on' might comprise a form of resistance because I had not yet obtained the necessary situational detail.

Later in the interview Nan mentioned that her boss was sometimes 'a big bully'. I asked how Nan responded to his bullying and learned that she sometimes followed him around the office, pestering him with trivial questions. She smiled as she said, 'Oh, yeah, he hates that.' This account suggested another perspective from which to view Nan's trip to Amsterdam. I asked Nan what had happened in Amsterdam after she found Chuck. 'Oh,' she said, 'we got back together but it only lasted three months.' She added casually, 'Then I left him.'

I had the sense that Nan had flown to Amsterdam less to be with Chuck than to retrieve her dignity. As this view differed sharply from the view Nan initially presented, I wanted to give her the chance to evaluate its suitability somewhat at a distance and so proposed it through an invented scenario. 'Can I ask you something? Imagine you and I are looking out of my office window. Across the street we see a young man and woman, yelling. Suddenly, the man punches the woman in the face. She hits the ground hard and sits there for a moment, stunned. Then he stomps off down the road. The woman gets up and runs after him, yelling at him to stop. Why? What is she after?' Nan thought for a moment and said, 'She can't let him just walk away like that.' 'Why not?' I asked. 'Well,' she said, 'she can't let him get away with that.' I then proposed, 'Could it be that you went to Amsterdam for the same reason? When Chuck hit you and then left, he took something important from you – your dignity as a person.' Nan overlapped, 'Yeah, my self-respect.' We smiled and nodded. I then went on, 'Could it be that you went to Amsterdam to get it back? And once you did, you no longer found it necessary to be with him?'

Nan then began to cry. She said, 'My God, I never thought of it like that. It feels like a huge weight has been lifted off my shoulders.' I continued, 'I agree that you're a cling-on. It seems that you cling to your self-respect for dear life – not to violent men. Also, from what you've told me, it seems like this condition is chronic. I'm pretty sure I won't be able to help you get over it.' I then asked a connective question: 'Have there been other times when you've had to preserve or reclaim your self-respect in this kind of way?' Nan went on to describe a number of related ways in which she had preserved her dignity and resisted disrespectful and abusive behaviour. We met five more times over a period of several months. Nan decided to stay with Bob for the time being as she did not want to traumatize Tom, who was very close to Bob. The important thing, she said, was that she knew she was 'not crazy'. Nan continued to assert herself more confidently in a manner that preserved her own and Tom's safety, while she planned her escape.

Conclusion

While violence cannot be reduced to a problem of language, neither can it be effectively addressed without accurate accounts of perpetrators' and victims' actions in specific instances. In legal and therapeutic settings language is often used in a manner that obscures the unilateral and deliberate nature of violent acts. Victims are widely represented as objects in a language of effects that conceals their responses and resistance to violence and other forms of adversity. As participants in this shared language, James and Nan initially presented their concerns as effects. The attributions 'I can't commit' and 'I'm a cling-on' presumed that they had submitted to violence and, in the process, had acquired lasting psychological problems (i.e. effects) that diminished their ability to address current difficulties.

But language is flexible and can be put to more judicious use, as Orwell's writing attests. The new and more accurate response-based accounts revealed that James resisted sexualized abuse and other forms of violence in childhood and, as an adult, devoted himself to a life of safety, respect and partnership with Sarah. Nan refused to adopt a submissive role in relation to men, even as a child, and later resisted physical and psychological abuse by two male partners. Like the girl in the slums, the despair James and Nan felt reflected their orientation to their circumstances as adverse. Response-based counselling does not replace collective efforts to address violence or other social problems but affirms individuals' despairing and hopeful responses as eminently practical forms of social action and expressions of human dignity.

Acknowledgement

Thanks to Imelda McCarthy, Nick Todd, Brenda Adams, Martine Renoux, Richard Routledge and Linda Coates for suggestions on earlier drafts of this chapter and to Tonya Gomes, Vikki Reynolds and Robin Routledge for many excellent conversations. The author can be contacted by e-mail at awade@cityu.edu, by phone at 250–701–0713 or by land mail at #216–80 Station St, Duncan BC, Canada, V9L 1M4.

References

Adams, B. (2005) Personal communication, 9 January.

Burstow, B. (1992) *Radical Feminist Therapy*. Newbury Park, CA: Sage.

Coates, L. (1996) The truth enslaved: anomalous themes in sexual assault trial judgments, paper presented at the Psychology Department, University of Birmingham, UK.

Coates, L. and Wade, A. (2004) Telling it like it isn't: obscuring perpetrator responsibility for violent crime, *Discourse and Society*, 15(5): 499–526.

Engel, B. (1990) *The Emotionally Abused Woman*. New York: Fawcett Columbine.

Fournier, S. and Crey, E. (1997) *Stolen From Our Embrace: The Abduction of First*

Nation's Children and the Restoration of Aboriginal Communities. Vancouver: Douglas & McIntyre.

Gomes, T. (2004) Response-based interviewing with women who engage in self-harm practices. Unpublished Masters thesis, City University of Vancouver.

Herman, J. (1997) *Trauma and Recovery.* New York: Basic Books.

hooks, bell (1990) Marginality as site of resistance, in R. Ferguson, M. Gever, T.T. Minh-ha and C. West (eds) *Out There: Marginalization and Contemporary Culture.* Cambridge, MA: MIT Press.

Kelly, L. (1988) *Surviving Sexual Violence.* Minneapolis, MN: University of Minnesota Press.

Lukacs, G. (1969) *Solzhenitsyn,* trans. William David Graf. London: Merlin Press.

McGee, D. (1999) How do therapeutic questions work? Unpublished doctoral dissertation, University of Victoria.

Milosz, C. ([1951] 1990) *The Captive Mind.* New York: Vintage International.

O'Neill, D. and Morgan, M. (2001) Pragmatic post-structuralism (I): participant observation and discourse in evaluating violence intervention, *Journal of Community and Applied Social Psychology,* 11(4): 263–75.

Orwell, G. (1937) *The Road to Wigan Pier.* Harmondsworth: Penguin.

Orwell, G. (1946) *Why I Write.* London: Penguin, 2004.

Orwell, G. (1949) *Nineteen Eighty-Four.* London: Secker & Warburg.

Orwell, G. (1952) 'Such, Such Were the Joys', *Partisan Review,* reprinted in S. Orwell and I. Angus (eds) *The Collected Essays, Journalism and Letters of George Orwell, Volume IV: In Front of Your Nose.* Harmondsworth: Penguin.

Reynolds, V. (2001) Personal communication, 11 November.

Scott, J.C. (1990) *Domination and the Arts of Resistance.* New Haven, CT: Yale University Press.

Shelden, M. (1991) *Orwell.* London: Heinemann.

Solzhenitsyn, A. (1968) *The First Circle.* London: William Collins & Harvill Press.

Todd, N. and Wade, A. (2003) Coming to terms with violence and resistance: from a language of effects to a language of responses, in T. Strong and D. Pare (eds) *Furthering Talk: Advances in the Discursive Therapies.* New York: Kluwer.

Todorov, T. (1990) *Facing the Extreme.* New York: Metropolitan.

Wade, A. (1997) Small acts of living: everyday resistance to violence and other forms of oppression, *Journal of Contemporary Family Therapy,* 19(1): 23–40.

Wade, A. (2000) Resistance to interpersonal violence: implications for the practice of therapy. Unpublished doctoral dissertation, University of Victoria.

Chapter 6

The getting and giving of wisdoms: generating hope

Catherine Ingram, Jenny, and Amaryll Perlesz

> Hope is something we do with others.
>
> (Weingarten 2000: 402)

> Hope is not contingent on outcome . . . Hope is relational in some deep, and enduring sense. It sits between us. It is sustained and nourished by memories, expectations, conversations and trust.
>
> (Maisel *et al.* 2004: 292)

Introducing the Wisdoms Project

The Wisdoms Project arose when we at Bouverie[1] reflected together that we were potentially sitting on a huge storehouse of clients' experiences that could be of interest to others who consult with the agency. Because we see so many families who experience a wide range of relational difficulties that are the effects of injury, abuse, illness and discrimination, we became excited by the idea of creating an archive of clients' wisdom narratives. Wisdom narratives, we believed, would tell the story of reconnecting to hope and well-being after traumatic and problem-saturated experiences. We were curious to learn what the effects on our clients would be to have access to such a collection. Thus a research project was born (see Ingram and Perlesz 2004). We defined wisdom as 'understanding that arises out of experience and supports and prepares one for future related experiences through ongoing reflection and learning'. For the purposes of the project, a narrative was understood as a piece of writing that articulates or expresses the author's thoughts, feelings, beliefs and experiences.

This chapter highlights the learnings from the Wisdoms Project and explores in depth the experiences of one client, Jenny, and her therapist, Catherine, who worked together in creating a wisdom narrative, and the impact of sharing those wisdoms with Jenny's own family, other therapists and other clients in an ongoing reflexive loop of 'doing hope' (Weingarten 2000).

Why a writing and story-telling project?

The healing effects of writing are multi-faceted. Writing has been shown to positively affect people's emotions, cognitions and physical well-being (Pennebaker 1997). Family therapists have also experimented with writing. David Nylund, in a survey of 40 families, found that therapeutic letters were worth 3.2 face-to-face interviews and that more than 50 per cent of the positive outcome of therapy was attributed to the letters alone (Nylund and Thomas 1994). David Epston has also established archives of written experiences by and for sufferers of anorexia, bulimia, obsessive compulsive disorder and other ailments, creating virtual communities of concern where 'insiders' support and share with each other the effects of the problem and counter-problem strategies (see *www.narrativeapproaches.com*).

Writing in therapy can create a 'dialogic' space between author as writer and author as listener to his or her own story, thus changing 'stuck' monologues into evolving dialogues and inviting changes in self-perception that influence changes in one's own and other family members' behaviour (Penn and Frankfurt 1994). People construct and alter their identities through language and the stories that they construct and tell about themselves and others (Schank 1990). Parables, fables and real-life stories have the potential to change the way we live our lives and relationships. We are therefore interested in locating people's knowledges in the world of experience and subjectivity, i.e. in their own stories or narratives – a subjectivity that brings forth agency and empowerment. The Wisdoms Project is an attempt to achieve this through the writing and reading process.

Painting ourselves into the picture

I (Catherine) embrace Buddhism as an important part of my life. Its teaching amounts to celebrating human life as a great, majestic and splendid jewel-studded tower that has infinite potential. New possibilities emerge when we engage, through thought, speech, feelings and actions with our preferred values, hopes, dreams, commitments and when we let these determine our direction. Our lives are deeply and fundamentally intertwined with the lives of others. To feel isolated, alone or stuck is life-destroying. 'I interact, therefore I am' sums up the Buddhist ethic of mutual coexistence. Thus it is that I am very hopeful when a family consults with me, for I believe each family member will have tucked away in some storyline the knowledges and abilities they need to overcome their problems.

In my (Amaryll's) work with people with head injuries and their families I have always grappled with the coexistence of hope and despair and how the complex stories of people's traumatic experiences shape their lives (Perlesz 1999). More recently I have attempted to give voice, pride and celebration to the generally subjugated and stigmatizing stories of marginalized people, particularly lesbians and their families (Perlesz and McNair 2004).

The Wisdoms Project provided us with an avenue to bring forward, in mutual co-creation and compassionate witnessing, unheard stories and knowledges, in order to engender hope. We see ourselves and those with whom we consult as doing hope together (Weingarten 2000). Those of us who participated in the research noticed this hope happening when people wrote or had their stories written for the Wisdoms Project. A virtuous cycle was made possible in having a story written that would be for others to hear and learn from, promoting the very thing we were trying to achieve in therapy – a healing experience and a sense of hope for both therapists and clients. It engendered not only a sense of belief or faith in the person's own abilities and wisdom to overcome suffering but also had the effect of generating a prideful and dignified sense of one's own worth, which invited the potentiality for ongoing change. Reading back the story to the author fostered self-compassion or love; a love which in turn rippled out to significant others in the person's family and community.

Jenny's story[2]

Jenny had been referred to Bouverie to get help with her increasingly violent children, and I (Catherine) met with her and three of her six children. The siblings' fighting was out of control. Fourteen-year-old Mark was wielding knives in rage and desperation. Fifteen years ago Jenny had finally been able to separate from the violent and abusive father of her first five children after eleven attempts to leave. Her three eldest children lived with their father.

There sat Jenny, clutching her shoulder bag tightly against her hip, stiff and wooden like an old piece of furniture that it might be dangerous to disturb. Words were hard to find. I was feeling the need to move gently. Jenny held that traumatized look of the headlighted rabbit, as she whispered to me, in broken words like shards of glass, that she could no longer go on, that her children would not listen to her, and there was nothing left for her to give. The countless holes in the walls of her home were testimony to everyone's rage and frustration, including her own. What to do?

Jenny later shared with me the anxiety that engulfed her:

I remember feeling very nervous and apprehensive about my first meeting . . . I had a kind of knot in my stomach and felt a bit nauseous, I was clutching my handbag the whole time . . . I felt very tense as I wasn't sure where or how I was going to start . . . was it going to be the same old story? I would see people, [painstakingly] tell my story and then they would have to stop seeing me and I would have to start over again.

Compassionate witnessing

As Jenny stood in the sculpture[3] with her children, Joe (12), Marie (15) and Mark (14), she looked overwhelmed. As she later explained, she could actually see, for the first time, just how isolated and separated from her children she had become. I also thought I heard and felt the children's sighs as they experienced a small release by this moment of truth. As Jenny said later: 'you got the kids to stand where they felt. That touched my heart so deeply. That's what I felt every day. I felt they were scattered. I didn't know how to find them.'

As I sat in this moment, I held onto that luminous space that lies between despair and hope, between dark and light; a recognition, within Jenny's tears, that something was missing but also that something was yearned for. Intuitively I sensed the possibility it held. That moment revealed to both of us that this powerful longing for something different was coming not only from Jenny but also from Marie – the daughter wanted closeness with her mother. She yearned for it. More tears fell as Jenny became a witness to this. So I suggested we begin our work together with mother and daughter. While dark and beautiful, Marie was mostly silent during our meetings. Her witnessing presence, and the intense moments of interest that lighted her face periodically, were indicators that we were on the right track.

From monologue to dialogue

It was not a smooth track, though, for the guilt and self-recrimination that tortured Jenny would so easily arise to obscure and block her way. Jenny wrote about the first session with her daughter:

I felt shy. It was the first time that I had been able to talk to my daughter – like mother and daughter. I was talking as if she and I had just met and that made me feel really sad . . . it showed how closed off emotionally and disconnected I had been with her for the 14 years of her life.

I wrote a letter in summary of the session we had had (the three of us). Jenny had acknowledged that the 'yelling and screaming' that she was desperately resorting to had the opposite effect to her intention to engender responsibility in her children and safety in the home. Her sadness was an expression of failure. She had failed herself as a mother who had only wanted to show care, love and consideration to her children. So I sent Jenny the letter that included these realizations and was taken aback when in the following session she said that the letter had made her feel worse. 'The letter is exposing,' she whispered. There was a long pause: 'Now people know I yell and scream and this makes me vulnerable . . . it's down on paper in black and white and it is there for everyone to see . . . I want to hide it . . . don't want people to read it.'

I had momentarily forgotten that one important finding from the Wisdoms Project research was that staying with the truth of one's experience and having this truth in writing can be enormously painful and challenging. One participant in the research put it like this:

I actually think you have to stay with the pain and the hurt and the horrible sense of loss and confusion and let it be part of who you are. I think that if you move too far away from the pain then you stay afraid of pain always and you also stay not knowing what the pain is really like.

The monologue that played in Jenny's head had been persecuting her: 'single-voiced, absolute and closed' (Penn and Frankfurt 1994: 223), and while the letter brought this voice into the open, initially shocking Jenny, it also made room for dialogue and for a more non-judgemental stance.

At that moment of moving from monologue to dialogue, something shifted for Jenny. After telling her story and hearing it read back, she wrote that she:

began to feel like I didn't want this past story to be in my emotional and mental system . . . to be in my life any more . . . to control me any more. I could take these papers and tear them up or even better, burn them . . . but I didn't do either. They are stored away in a file I will probably keep forever more. The demon is no longer there to haunt me.

Writing invites disclosures

I persevered, determined to have Jenny's story and wisdom in writing, if she would allow it, for I truly believed that the woman sitting in front of me was sitting on valuable wisdom. I 'doubly listened' (White 2004) as we explored together the history of Jenny's preference for love and care in her relationships, concurrently with the hurt, suffering, loss and guilt that had dogged her life. It took a while before Jenny was openly talking and writing about her past history of abuse. Like the participants in the Wisdoms Project, the effect of writing and hearing back enabled Jenny to share more, and me to witness more.

I was to learn through this process how Jenny and her twin sister, who subsequently suicided, and her four other siblings, had endured sexual, physical and emotional abuse from their father for years. I learned that the profound effects of these experiences for Jenny were not only the unbearable loss of her twin to prostitution, self-mutilation and death and the ensuing grief, but also the painful witnessing of the effects on her brothers of the abuse: mental illness, alcoholism, anxiety, panic attacks. Jenny herself was admitted to a psychiatric institution twice.

More compassionate witnessing

I asked myself: 'How will I render back to Jenny what I am experiencing in my conversations with her? If I am doing hope with her my witnessing cannot be taken lightly. How will I capture the shape of her words, the colour and texture of her depictions, such that the reality of her experience is heard compassionately?' There is fear and risk for me. How can I hold this sacred space with Jenny and reflect back what I see as her wisdom and strength? I hold Kaethe Weingarten's witnessing theory close to my heart as I intend to find the space where we are both 'empowered and aware'. Jenny's heroism moves me, though I wondered if Jenny herself was aware of her heroic abilities. Apparently not! Jenny needed to recognize this, as others needed to hear and witness this universal story – the familiar and at the same time unique story of a woman's experience of abuse and violence.

A story in writing

We decided together to co-author a letter from Jenny to her daughter. This letter would be for Marie, for mothers and daughters who experience and have experienced the effects of domestic violence, and for the Bouverie Wisdoms archive.[4]

The narratives in the Bouverie archive have been written in a number of ways – by the protagonists in their own time and of their own volition, ghost-written by the therapist following a post-therapy interview, and ghost-written by the therapist (in first or third person) as the therapy progressed (Ingram and Perlesz 2004). I wrote down Jenny's words verbatim during each session, as I questioned her about her understandings and experiences, and then I put these into a first-person narrative to read back to Jenny after two or three sessions. As an ethnographer and 'participant researcher' I charted with curiosity and wonder Jenny's rich 'practitioner researcher's' journey (Epston 1999). As we researched together, we learned together. Jenny discovered what she knew but had not yet voiced or found words for. She found herself to be, like so many of the participants in the research project, amazed at her own wisdom and ability. Now it was out in black and white for all to see. There was now no denying this wisdom and its effects: 'Wow, amazing, I can't believe I said all that. It is unbelievably true, a revelation . . . somewhere in there, in my life, I always felt this wisdom, like it's been there all these years since I was 12 years old.'

A journey from shame to pride

Jenny's sense of pride in having a narrative worthy of being written, was palpable:

The difference of seeing your story down on paper rather than just talking about it is that you feel like you really are being heard, you don't feel
fobbed off. You begin to feel like you are important in this world and not
just someone walking around with a story stuck in their head . . . Your
story feels more important than anyone else's when you see it in words on
paper . . . I don't feel ashamed, I don't feel guilty any more. I am me. The
guilt and self-hate that I had, stopped me from getting to know who I
really was.

The participants of the Wisdoms Project had told us that helping someone else can lead to an added change in self-perception which comes from
believing they have a 'success' story to offer. Jenny was changing before my
eyes: colour came to her cheeks, strength and music and excitement could be
heard in her voice. She was no longer a victim of a terrible story; she was a
hero who had something to offer the world. Jenny's hope and healing had
been enhanced by a recognition that her story was worthy to be told, and that
her life was a cause for rejoicing. The story had become a gift, the storyteller a
giver, to struggling others.

Self-compassion

This process was also giving Jenny a significantly different view of herself –
one that contained self-love and appreciation. Hearing one's own story as an
'externalized' narrative (in the first or third person) enables the person to
separate enough so that she can see herself as she would another in the same
position. She becomes a compassionate witness to herself and is able to let go
of her monologue of rigid self-deprecation and self-punitive perfectionism
that abuse perpetrated on the self by another can invite. She enters into the
creative space of dialogue. Buddhist theory has it that a person who can
embrace herself in such a way, with a warm heart, with compassion, can
invite courage. This courage can turn despair into hope and self-forgiveness,
as Jenny found:

I feel that I have found that inner confidence that I had as a young girl . . .
It was taken away from me through all the abuse that I endured . . . the
guilt and the self-hate that I had, stopped me from getting to know who
I really was . . . I have more forgiveness and love for myself now than
guilt . . . guilt just made me feel like I was a bad person. With forgiveness
I can say to myself, 'you can change that'.

Retrieving autobiographical memory

Michael White (2004) has drawn on Russell Meares' findings (2000) related to
the effects of trauma on memory, and demonstrated the healing effects of the

re-authoring process on the memory system. The autobiographical and epi-sodic memory of a person who has experienced moderate and recurring trauma is affected such that the person's sense of 'this is me' eludes them. The abuse Jenny had experienced as a child and then as an adult had this effect, but the process of developing a written narrative that is meaningful, whole, congruent and unifying, reconnected Jenny to her 'me' and her sense of 'myself'. She was able to experience her 'self' as present, aware, feeling good and no longer hurt or traumatized: 'Before, I looked in the mirror and I saw a person but I didn't know who she was. I wasn't connected . . . I am accepting myself, liking myself, to the point of loving myself.'

Virtuous cycles of compassion

According to Buddhist theory, too, it is only when we have been able to embrace our own lives that we can truly cherish others in their suffering, embracing it as our own. In the change of self-perception that a wisdom narrative engenders comes a change in perception of others. On the day we had decided to read the completed letter to Marie, Jenny had been feeling very nervous. After the reading she said:

I couldn't tell Marie what I felt before because I was scared of being vulnerable, not knowing what she was feeling or thinking – maybe nega-tive things. Now I feel we have the connection and the trust. It has been a journey to know me and my daughter. I feel Marie looks at me in a different way. Before, it felt like she was over the mountains, too far away . . . I was a piece of cardboard walking around, a stick figure doing chores. Before, it was like she was afraid to go near me, touch me. Now it feels like I am fully there and she can look at me and feel how I care for her. Now she hears me, I can see it in her face. I cuddle her when she is upset. It is like I have put a plug in the socket and we have connected. The power has been connected. I am now a flesh and blood person with feelings and emotions . . . and I can support her.

Jenny has come far since the day she sat in front of me, with her children, a broken shell. The changes are not only with how she relates to Marie, as Jenny's boys are also responding positively to Jenny's changes:

I used to yell for them to do anything. I would get very angry. I knew I was hurting them. Then I started looking inside myself and thought I wouldn't like to be yelled at like that. I realized I had to change myself; respect myself. When Mark started pulling knives, I see now it was a cry for help. I remembered when I was 13 or 14 I knew that there was some-thing my mother wasn't doing for me, and I thought 'I am never going to do that to my kids'. And then I was hearing her voice in my voice, her actions in my actions. I was exactly like my mother. I hated it so much I decided to stop . . . when I changed my way with Marie she changed her way with her brothers. She stopped being nasty to them when I stopped being nasty to her. Before they couldn't be in the same room without fighting, now, would you believe, they cook me dinner together and let me have time out when I ask for it!

Jenny is very clear that the love she has garnered for herself has brought forward the love she has for her children, and enabled her to connect with them in a way her mother was never able to do with her. The reflective process and ritual of telling, writing, listening to the writing and retelling was a defining event in Jenny's life. It meant that Jenny could change the mother–child story that had been passed down to her and live in her preferred way.

The giving

The stories in our Wisdoms Archive contain elements of encouragement, practical ideas, ambiguity and excitement that capture, as well as invite, the possibility for change in the listener (Frantz 1995). Stories read out to our clients are chosen because of their resonance with other clients' narratives and lives. In this vein, I shared Jenny's letter to Marie with Marion and her daughter. Marion had experienced domestic violence by the father of her two children. Like Jenny, she had left her violent husband and, like Jenny, she was experiencing violence from her son, but the difference was that the violence was directed towards Marion and not towards his sister.

I read the letter in front of Marion and her 15-year-old daughter, Amy, and then they took the letter home. Marion said she felt the urge to read and reread it several times. The letter had invited her to reflect more deeply on her own experience of living with a violent man. She identified with much that Jenny had described: head in a fog; slow and steady loss of sense of self and one's own power; self-neglect; over-responsibility for others; lack of connection with and awareness of her own children's thoughts and feelings; and dismay and regret for not being able to leave earlier. Marion spoke adamantly and with a newly found confidence in the next session: 'I will never allow anyone to take the power away from me again, because I am an assertive person, I can make good decisions. I am a loyal person, honest and caring . . . I allowed my spirit to be killed, it was soul destroying.'

Marion was also glad to have her daughter hear the letter, 'because then she knows our experience is not strange'. Marion wanted Amy to know that her mother was not a freak and their family was not abnormal. Amy too felt empowered after reading the letter: 'When I have had enough I stand up for my rights and other people's rights and the right thing. I want to treat others how I would like to be treated.'

The virtuous cycle continues

Jenny sounded flat the day I phoned to give her Marion and Amy's feedback following their reading of Jenny's wisdom. As I began to share the striking effects of her letter, Jenny's voice sounded lighter: 'That is unbelievable,' she exclaimed, 'that is so good.' When we finished the conversation, I said to Jenny: 'Have a good weekend.' Suddenly her voice had the ring of golden bells: 'I sure will now!'

A month earlier I had read to Jenny the written responses to the reading of her letter to over 40 professionals at a family therapy research seminar. She told me this one was her favourite:

Jenny, you have a lot of courage in sharing your story with us. It is inspirational and I feel very moved by your letter. I am reminded of the importance of accepting the idea, 'you are your own best friend'. This is something I have been thinking about for some time and also struggling with . . . a lot of people who have seen me have struggled with this too. Your story has also connected me with our own power as a mother and how guilt can undermine this. Thank you.

Other clients' and professionals' responses to her letter have given Jenny further confirmation of her own wisdom.

Concluding thoughts

The experiences we have had in the research project of reading back others' wisdoms reinforces for us the power of human connection in engendering hope. We do 'do hope' together. The story invites the reader or listener to engage in an experience and to relate this to his or her own life. When we hear a story with an ending that relates wisdom, the understanding that comes from experience, we are potentially inspired and hope is generated. We also feel connected and no longer isolated in our suffering. The stories in the archive are something akin to modern-day parables. They can have the same encouraging and enlightening effect as a parable for the reader/listener. Within the particular, the universal can be heard. As one Bouverie client wrote in response to a story from the Wisdoms archive: 'You touched my heart in a big way and thank you for sharing your courageous story . . . In healing yourself there was a part of me that was healed forever.'

We have found that making the wisdom narratives available in the Bouverie Centre's waiting room, and using them in therapy, creates a type of self-help group – connecting through experiential knowledge, but in this case virtually. David Epston is convinced that 'the stories from the insiders are incomparable to the stories written about them by outsiders' (Epston *et al.* 1995: 299). The experiences of self-compassion created through telling, writing, reading, listening to and bearing witness to one's own and others' stories are not dissimilar to experiences reported by clients and therapists involved in multiple family groups, reflecting teams and outsider witness groups. There is a profound sense of not being alone, being heard and moving from shame to pride. When Marion and Amy listened to Jenny's story, they no longer felt or experienced being 'strange'. They belonged to a community. They felt understood. Suddenly Marion could see that psychologists and helpers she had consulted with in the past had often invited confusion. No one could reach or affect her in the way Jenny did. Not only that, now she was motivated to write her own story! The reflexive loop of 'doing hope' is an ongoing journey.

Acknowledgements

Catherine Ingram would like to thank firstly the Wisdoms research group (Dr Amaryll Perlesz, Nicky Maheras, Pam Rycroft, Greg U'ren, Dr Colin Reiss and Dr Jenny Dwyer) who back in 2000 gave of themselves over and above their already heavy work schedules so that this project was made possible. Secondly, the families, and Jenny and her family in particular, who in giving their stories to struggling others have enriched the journey of many who come to the Bouverie Centre. And lastly, Amaryll, whose trust and faith in me has allowed Wisdoms to go places we never would have imagined.

Notes

1 The Bouverie Centre is a publicly funded family therapy centre in Melbourne, Australia.
2 Jenny's full story and all letters written in therapy are available on the Bouverie website: www.latrobe.edu.au/bouverie.
3 Family members had been asked to create a sculpture and to position themselves spatially in relation to each other.
4 The full letter is on the Bouverie Wisdoms website – www.latrobe.edu.au/bouverie.

References

Epston, D. (1999) Co-research: the making of an alternative knowledge, in *Narrative Therapy and Community Work: a Conference Collection*, pp. 137–57. Adelaide: Dulwich Centre Publications.
Epston, D., White, M. and 'Ben' (1995) Consulting your consultants, in S. Friedman (ed.) *The Reflective Team in Action*. New York: Guilford Press.
Epston, D. and White, M. (1990) Consulting your consultants. the documentation of alternative knowledges, in D. Epston and M. White (eds) *Experience, Contradiction, Narrative and Imagination*. Adelaide: Dulwich Centre Publications.
Frantz, T.G. (1995) Stories for therapy: the right story to the right person at the right time, *Contemporary Family Therapy*, 17, 1: 47–64.
Freeman, J., Epston, D. and Lobovits, D. (1997) *Playful Approaches to Serious Problems*. New York: W.W. Norton.

Ingram, C. and Perlesz, A. (2004) The getting of Wisdoms, *International Journal of Narrative Therapy and Community Work*, Issue Number 2: 49–56.

Maisel, R., Epston, D., Borden, A. (2004) *Biting the Hand that Starves You*. New York: Norton.

Meares, R. (2000) *Intimacy and Alienation: Memory, Trauma and Personal Being*, London: Routledge.

Nylund, D. and Thomas, J. (1994) The economics of narrative, *Family Therapy Networker*, 18(6): 38–9.

Penn, P. and Frankfurt, M. (1994) Creating a participant text: writing, multiple voices, narrative multiplicity, *Family Process*, 33(3): 217–31.

Pennebaker, J.W. (1997) *Opening Up: The Healing Power of Expressing Emotion*. New York: Guilford Press.

Perlesz, A. (1999) Complex responses to trauma: challenges in bearing witness, *Australian and New Zealand Journal of Family Therapy*, 20(1): 11–19.

Perlesz, A. and McNair, R. (2004) Lesbian parenting: insiders' voices, *Australian and New Zealand Journal of Family Therapy*, 25(2): 129–40.

Schank, R.C. (1990) *Tell Me a Story: A New Look at Real and Artificial Memory*. New York: Charles Scribner & Sons.

Weingarten, K. (2000) Witnessing, wonder and hope, *Family Process*, 39(4): 389–402.

White, M. (2004) Working with people who are suffering the consequences of multiple trauma: a narrative perspective, *The International Journal of Narrative and Community Work*, 1: 45 76.

Chapter 7

Finding a way towards being

Suzanne Shuda and Just Anna

> It is as if the stuff of which we are made were totally transparent and therefore imperceptible and as if the only appearances of which we can be aware are cracks and planes of fracture in that transparent matrix.
>
> (Bateson 1979: 15)

Introduction

The work presented in this chapter was developed over a period of five years. Initially our conversations were about Anna's desperation and wanting to kill herself. We began to search for some points of light in what seemed to be endless darkness and despair. Anna chose some of the important moments in our conversations as well as some poetry to share in this chapter.

My (SS) relationship with hope started while growing up on a farm and being part of the planting of crops and the hoping for rain. When it rained, the drops were received and allowed hope to grow. We then waited patiently for the germination of seed and the tender shoots to appear. The possibility of drought was always present with its inevitable consequences: despair and hopelessness.

The natural cycle of the earth through the seasons continues to be a guide as I work, listening to people and the stories of their lives. A young man I knew sent me a picture of a lily, which only blooms after fire has devastated an area. Seeing the picture of this lily filled me with wonder and appreciation for the conversations in which people share the devastation in their lives. Together we search through ashes for small traces. Sometimes we find a 'fire lily'.

Working with despair becomes possible if we can understand the danger of models and the desire for certainty but still begin to create a rare environment of discovery (Bird 2000: ix). This discovery happens through a commitment to understanding people and skilfully utilizing language as the link between us (Bakker and Shuda 1989).

Johnella Bird, in writing about therapy and navigating life's contradictions, says:

dominant discourses reside most comfortably within ideas, thus saturating people's (clients') thinking. When we negotiate the meanings attributed to significant life events by utilising the resources of ideas, feelings and the body, we access a richer tapestry of potential meanings. In these moments we can find ourselves engaging with issues of morality, life and death.

(2000: 18)

She continues: 'A betrayal of faith can damage the spirit to the extent that there appears only one choice available and that is to disengage from life' (p. 20). Bird goes on to suggest a mechanism by which such dominant discourses provide a ground on which hopelessness can flourish.

To continue to move away from the fixed representation of people's experience has been an ongoing professional and personal challenge for me. For instance, reading *about* people's lives, as professionally or clinically documented by another writer, is intolerable to me at the moment. It seems of vital importance that the world somehow takes note of how we all become deadened by dominant discourses about clinical practices. If writing will not allow the voice of the person to be present in its raw form, how will we address the issue of wanting to disengage from life? My attempt to keep despair and hopelessness at bay is simply to try to listen carefully to each word. However, when writing, the dilemma is how to avoid the trap that I have been describing above. One way is to attempt to acknowledge the other as clearly and directly as 'professionalism' will allow. Without this I am unable to begin to find words for my attempts at being useful in conversing with others.

The first meeting

Suzanne's story

Anna walked into my office with downcast eyes and her shoulders hanging. She appeared very distressed and withdrawn. She sat next to a chair in a crouched position on the floor, rocking to and fro. At times she would pull pieces of wool from the mat and roll them between her fingers. Her desperation seemed very deep. Words seemed inappropriate. I crouched opposite her and offered her my hands. Anna did not look up but reached out and held my hands. I gripped her wrists firmly and gently supported her rocking movements. I softly asked if this was OK with her. When she made eye contact, I asked if she felt comfortable. She nodded. After a while, Anna asked for a cigarette and got up to smoke outside the office. We began to speak of what she needed to continue feeling comfortable.

Anna's story

At this time I was completely, but completely lost. I had a roof over my head, but did not feel contained at all. I had been discharged from a mental hospital using a huge amount of will-power to get myself out of an extremely damaging situation. The hospital was terrifying and no voice from any 'patient' was ever heard. I had no option but to keep out of hospital no matter what. My family seemed to have no idea what was going on and did not want to interfere with the doctors' 'treatment'. I had only myself to fall back on which was very difficult as I hated myself. Every word, every person, every situation seemed to pierce me to the quick and I was all too ready to throw myself away. I did not know who I should become. Could I become anyone? Or had my life been working towards this disposal? The world was happening out there and I could not connect to anything to make me part of it. As the situation got worse I realized that my pain was beyond belief and I phoned a friend for help and went to stay with her for some months.

This friend believed in me enough for me to begin to take a grip on myself. This was a very, very low point in my life. She took me to Suzanne who reached out to me and slowly extracted a tiny splinter of hope. With faith she gave me goals each week that got me to believe that the extreme effort required would be of worthwhile consequence.

Anna's family (Suzanne)

Since the age of 17 Anna had been hospitalized several times. Her parents, both converts to Catholicism, had strong anti-apartheid feelings. Anna was one of six children. Other siblings suffered from anxiety and depression. Their father had a fine intellect with which he was able to make ideas visible but also with which he plunged into severe depressions and highs difficult to keep up with. When Anna was 3 her father had a breakdown and the children were placed in a children's home for a 'very damaging three weeks'. Anna became a 'difficult child'. Her mother had no option but to cope and this she did at great expense to herself. Fear and insecurity reigned. Working against the government was tough. The phone was tapped, the special branch had their eyes on the family and at times activists were hidden in their home. When Anna was 16, her brother committed suicide. At 26 years of age, Anna had her own son who is now an adult.

Anna: my diary

I began with a diary, it was very, very bleak, but at least I had the diary and the diary was me. At least it was there, it was readable and re-readable and could be viewed as a collection of old bones, perhaps a skeleton on which I discovered fragments of flesh and these gradually took hold and more substance began to emerge. This was a very important process. I had something to hold on to. Daily accounts of how I felt and what I was doing. Some days I would stay in bed for most of the time, vomiting and then sitting up just to write. And the next day it was there to see. I had so much physical apprehension and suffered severely from dizziness. I did not know if I could ever overcome the thoughts about suicide. I wanted to beat and scratch myself. I got excited when I thought of taking an overdose. I felt a gun might be the best way.

Loneliness – by Anna
Corpses lace
the dead end streets
city of my nativity

Ancestors beckon
deepthroated hollow echoes
film my frame with silted dust.
I clamber a-top a lamp a-flame
Do you or anyone know my name?

The theme of death (Suzanne)

Death was the main theme of Anna's diary at that time of our initial meetings and seemed to be the only option for Anna. She felt that her family did not want her, that she could not look after herself and that she could not live on her own. We spoke about the experiences that had brought her to this conclusion. We reflected on her different admissions to psychiatric hospitals. Trying to find herself and who she could possibly be without the identity of a psychiatric patient invited Anna into the unknown. Johnella Bird (2000: 317) describes this as disconnection and 'in the corner' ideas. There was also a deafening and overwhelming chorus encouraging the 'disconnection' (Bird 2000: 320). The unique outcome (White and Epston 1990) was that Anna did not want to go back to a mental hospital.

In my first discussion with the psychiatrist, he mentioned how thick her files were and that Anna was well known to the hospital authorities over many years. She had had several diagnoses, the most frequent being bipolar disorder. The family dynamics had never been explored and he warned me against any form of psychotherapy that would open up more of Anna's experiences. We had an agreement to meet and Anna's mother was also invited to some of the meetings. These meetings were new to the psychiatrist especially since I insisted on Anna being present throughout and on us documenting our discussions. After our second meeting I also asked Anna to write an account of the meeting from her memory and assisted her with the notes I had taken. She added her comments and reflections.

Anna and I met alone weekly and began to discuss her diary filled with her hospital experiences. This was harrowing. I tried to be an appropriate witness, mostly at a loss for words and overwhelmed by the pain and disqualification that she had experienced. We had to find a way of 'breathing life into her words' (Bird 2000: 27) and I knew I had to hold the possibility of life and hope.

Reflection on hospital

Anna's story

One needs a lot of time to recover from the shock of being in a hospital. I know what it is like to be in those wards. I know I will feel even worse if I have to go back. I have slit my wrists, tried to suffocate myself, and hang myself. I once tried to strangle myself with a surgical glove. I remember ill people and buckets of urine. I remember trying to drink water out of a toilet. I once ran away out of a locked ward, I squeezed out through a broken window and went to the police. I was taken back the next day. We were treated like cattle. I was the only white person and there was an inverse racism going on. People were often beaten up. I used to take a rock and hit myself on the head. I felt so utterly worthless. One of the night nurses told me that there were many terrible things written in my file that they all knew about. I am even scared to think of it now. I never felt that I was taken seriously, I was observed, judged and written off. I stayed in hospital because my family could not have me back home. My mother used to say that I made my father worse.

Now I am really trying to change this pattern, staying out of hospital. I am developing outlets, ways of coping that are feasible within the community. I have a few people who recognize the pain. They don't deny it. They can see how bad it is, take cognizance. Then I can move on. I need people to recognize it.

I would like people to know that people in hospital have feelings whether they are psychotic or not. They cannot be treated like animals. I do not know why some of the staff are in the caring profession. I am convinced that they do not care. I was a totally harmless patient. I was made to feel that I was attention-seeking. I withdrew completely and I did not know who I was by the end. I want you to know that even the maddest person has feelings. I was never allowed to question anything.

I feel so small
I feel so vulnerable and dependent
I feel so scared and want to resume
an endless sleep.

Our first reflecting team meeting (Suzanne)

I needed new ideas to work with Anna's integrity and to create alternatives (Andersen 1987). I knew the transformative potential (White 1995: 176) of reflecting teamwork and suggested to Anna that we meet with a team I had been working with. Anna was initially apprehensive due to her experiences of ward rounds. I explained to her that she would be assessing the value of the work done with the team and that there would be no further diagnosis. We agreed to video our meetings so that we could process the discussions in our own time.

A team member writes a letter to Anna

Dear Anna,

After the meeting with you I thought of some questions that I would have liked to ask you and I also wanted to offer you some of my reflections on the notes I had taken while you and Suzanne were speaking.

Firstly, you said that you felt that everyone had denied your experiences in the past. That is, until you started talking to Suzanne, you said this has made your experiences real because she listens and has given you words to hold onto.

You said that it feels as if you have learned something from the last 26 years and that they have not been a complete waste of time. This made me wonder if there are other things or learnings that also add to the meaningfulness of the past 26 years.

You mentioned that a friend recognizes that you have taken a big stand to get to where you are today. Can you think of other people who may also recognize this? If your friend were able to talk to us, what might she say about you taking these big steps? Do you think this is something that she or other people might have noticed about you before? I don't really know if this question is helpful, if it does not make sense please don't worry about it.

You spoke about being so grateful about departing from some of the ways your family saw you in the past and said that you have been trying to give yourself recognition for your efforts. And you said that you do recognize now that you do have a future. Who else do you think knows this or has noticed this?

You mentioned that a lot of your passion comes from injustice and that while you felt that wisdom is a kitsch word you could not think of a better one to describe what you meant when you said that you were a bit 'ancient' in your perspective. I was struck on numerous occasions while you and Suzanne were talking by your wisdom about justice and injustice, your realization that 'I have a right to be here, I've kept my sense of this even when I was in the hospital'.

I wonder how you have managed to hold onto your strength. The words brave, not giving up, persevering, courage, tenacious, creative, resourceful come to mind.

Anna, your conversation was a reminder to me as a therapist to always be accountable for my actions and words, to be real and genuine and to acknowledge the other person as a person in their own right. I hope I have heard you and I want to carry this message with me in my work.

I remember you saying that you wish you could have taken notes, so I have tried to capture as much as I could of what you said. I hope this can be of some use to you.

Many thanks,

Jenny

The team were struck by Anna's courage and determination to change her life. Giving up was not something that came naturally to Anna. She was committed to finding an alternative identity, focusing on what made her feel good and how she could act to ensure growth in this preferred direction.

Following up on the team meeting, Anna remembered that while in hospital she had been told that she was not well enough to benefit from therapy. The team reflections were very different from her experiences of meetings in the hospital.

The hospital file (Suzanne)

We decided that it would be valuable for Anna to have access to the dreaded hospital file. Anna was admitted to hospital in 1976 for the first time. Her fear about the knowledge in the file continued to undermine her. She wanted to know what the 'bad side' of her was and this seemed connected to the file. She wanted to start a new life and stay out of hospital, but she doubted herself. Would this always overcome her and how would she put doubt into the past? How would she stop the horrible memories from haunting her? Her diary was filled with blackness and reasons for ending her life.

I wrote to the hospital authorities requesting a copy of the file. With the new South African constitution this had been made possible. Special permission was granted, by the superintendent, to give us access to her file. We waited anxiously as the necessary correspondence was processed and we finally received an answer that we could now view to the file.

Anna accompanied me on the journey to the hospital to collect her file. The superintendent handed us less than 100 copied pages with admissions only since 1994 and a note that Anna had had many admissions. The superintendent was curious about my interest and wanted to know what we hoped to achieve.

Anna's response

From Anna: I am trying to recover from all their thinking about me. If someone thinks I will be OK then I will be all right but as soon as they start thinking and not sharing that, there is a mystery, that there is all this stuff that only they as professionals can see, then I get terribly anxious.

We had 'the stuff that only professionals could see' in our hands. Anna and I began reading the file. It had far less content than she had expected. Her memory was of continually being written about. The file contained the details of some of the most difficult parts of her life. Anna remembered three files being wheeled in on a trolley for case discussions, a history hard to leave behind her, following her into every new admission, being used as an important reference point in every discussion with or about her. Here it was, safely in her hands. Anna could read and then decide to save it, shred it, burn it or throw it away. Anna's initial apprehension gave way to outrage. We read faster and faster and then just jumped forward through the entries, catching diagnoses and descriptions of her behaviour here and there. At times Anna spoke of events and her memories of them. Suddenly Anna sat back, laughed and said: 'The file says nothing. *Nothing* about who I am or of what has happened to me. They never knew who I was, what I thought or what I felt. They knew nothing! These are just their words. I am somebody else.' Anna was amazed and relieved from the idea that '*the file*' had had such importance in her life.

> **Beyond the Inkblot – by Anna**
> The audacity
> of casual interference
> observed behavioural parameters
> mapped with grid imposed
> affective phenomena, chemical fixes, iron cast.
> Ambiguity and ambience
> lambasted
> roots ripped.
> as an 'authority'
> drives home the crippling nail:
> you are not whole
> your core and pips are sterile
> we've laced your tea with niceties
> but take umbridge
> at your authenticity

Anna's son (Suzanne)

Working with the contents of the file seemed to release Anna to explore other parts of her life. Two of the important alternative stories in Anna's life were her relationship with her son and a dress she wore when she was a child. Anna had managed to be a good mother in spite of being hospitalized. Anna remembered being very anxious as a small child and could not talk to her mother. These memories created an awareness with which she approached her relationship with her son. The other sparkling alternative was the dress. I asked her to draw it and we had many conversations about the time when she wore this dress and the way she experienced herself.

Anna's story of motherhood

From the moment my son was born, he knew what he wanted. He had no trouble filtering out information, while I always felt, and still feel, bombarded. The minute I knew that I was pregnant, I gave up smoking. I saw a nutritional expert and lived on vitamins and yoghurt. I worried that I may not cope with the birth and I lost a lot of blood. I was scared that he may have a cleft palate or be autistic, but he was beautiful. He had sweet eyes and a little dark downy hair. He grew fatter, faster and fitter and I faded away. I made sure always to be there for him and held in there for him. When I was in hospital I always used to try and think of ways to earn a little bit of money so that I would be able to get him a gift for his birthday or at Christmas. I have always told him that he is wonderful. When I was a student I won two class medals and my father never came to the ceremony. I have treated him very differently to how I felt had been treated. I put him first, always first. I had no prescription for him but let him explore the world and develop his own relationship with it. He is now married, at university and has a deep love of life and knowledge. He climbs, paints, writes and most of all, he knows himself.

As a child we were left to ourselves too much and there was a lot of sibling rivalry. We were not managed properly. My mother was scared of teenagers and erratic. I was teased about sexuality and my mother freaked out about it. I always try to set my son at ease and give him the warmth and love I did not receive.

Joint conversations on Anna's motherhood (Suzanne)

We began to speak about the way Anna had held on to her warmth in spite of being in hospital and how she had decided to be a mother to her son. She knitted a blue jersey with orange triangles for him while in hospital and felt it was a privilege to be asked for things by him. Anna had used her awareness of her childhood to bring to their relationship the qualities she felt were important to assist him to feel confident and safe in the world. It was important for her that he had his own voice from a very young age. She wanted him to discover the world for himself and experience his mastery through that. Anna had a keenly developed idea of how this sense of oneself can be taken away. Her son excelled academically and was a source of tremendous pride. Anna knew what her attempts had been to mother him in spite of her being hospitalized. This became a strong foothold from which we could work. Anna felt the least scared to be herself with him and knew that she had made an important contribution to his life.

After one year Anna was writing the reports of our joint meetings. She had set goals for the next year and was beginning to talk more about who she was, not the psychiatric patient, but being a mother, her interest in her artwork, her love of writing, animals and creating a home for herself and her brother with whom she was sharing a flat. She had begun to create her own place in the world where she felt safe and happy. Anna found books on ancient African designs and began experimenting with making cards.

After the second reflecting team meeting: Anna's story

To watch the video was an absolutely wonderful experience for me. It left me feeling pretty good about who I am. I am no longer 'attempting' to survive, but I am surviving and the possibilities to enrich and enliven my daily existence do exist. It was clear that I felt very safe with everyone and that I could be honest and sincere. I was not being exploited, but was given a chance to articulate and see more clearly for myself. I think what has been most helpful was seeing myself really, as myself, and liking myself. There was no one correcting me, tempering me, reprimanding or ignoring me. They were professional people, they believed in me, not like the professionals at the hospital who were sceptical and critical of me. In one word, I felt respected. I was with people who really listened and really understood and this helped me to say things I have longed to say, to help both myself and others. The focus on me did not feel 'too much' or in any way intrusive. I found the questions challenging and they made things clearer. I have found my life extremely difficult. If what I have battled through and with can help others to take courage, I think my life would have been worthwhile. The knowledge that one knows one is speaking the truth and this time is actually believed: therein lies the healing power of therapy.

I felt I came across as a positive force as opposed to a negative one, and yet I felt I was me. The surprise conclusion therefore was that I am a positive force. Thank you for believing in me from the first time we met when I could hardly talk for fear and the problem seemed insurmountable. You have been a constant thread running through my life since we met. You have helped me get a disability grant and copyright my cards and you have seen me getting a part-time job for the first time. I am living in a loving environment where people are believing in me and trusting me – my son bears no grudges towards me and without him it would have been hard to soldier on. I definitely would never like to hurt him . . . he wants me to take care. This video goes a long way with helping me want to take care and respect myself.

Conclusion (Suzanne)

A disability grant requires a lengthy application requiring submissions on income, expenditure, letters verifying financial support, in Anna's case also a letter from her ex-husband stating his financial support for their son, as well as medical reports and treatment history. Once Anna had decided that she was entitled to this support, she managed to complete the whole process very quickly.

An appointment was made for Anna to discuss her African Ink card-making idea and make sure she held the copyright and would be acknowledged for this work.

In 2003 Anna completed a course in oral history and media through the Human Rights Media Centre. The course was offered to help people to create and present their stories of survival. They also interviewed persons with similar dilemmas and compared stories and themes. At the final presentation to a large audience, Anna wore a cap and used it to award herself a degree at the end of her talk. It was done with humour, illustrations and a lot of useful information about living with bipolar disorder.

Since 1999 Anna has had two hospitalizations lasting less than a month. One of the special things Anna and I became aware of was that if she did not take a holiday or go away for a while, she ended up in hospital over the Christmas period. A new cycle developed where Anna worked on producing cards to sell in December. She also began to make arrangements to spend some time out of her routine, going away at the end of the year.

Anna is currently living in Cape Town with her mother and is a sought-after caretaker of young and old. She has a dog called Daisy who was abandoned and who has become attached, loyal, playful and friendly. Anna and Daisy love to go on walks. She continues to write poetry and make cards under the name of African Ink. We still meet once a fortnight to talk about her life and to write.

White and Epston (1990: 13) see the evolution of lives as 'akin to the process of reauthoring, the process of persons' entering into stories, taking them over and making them their own'. In their view an acceptable outcome for those seeking therapy would be the generation of alternative stories that will allow them to perform new meanings, which they 'will experience as more helpful, satisfying and open-ended' (White and Epston (1990: 15). Anna and I met in a time of despair for her. Together we negotiated foreign territory

(Bird 2000: 324) that has brought us both to believe that it is possible to find hope from places of utmost despair. Anna the psychiatric patient is now Anna the mother, artist, caretaker, student and writer, and more dimensions of her life continue to evolve.

Anna's closing

Trust and love are truly what is most needed in this world. For me, it was this trust that was broken in my early years that affected me severely. But, with a fantastic amount of care and attention, I have turned back from the point of no return. I now inhabit a world in which I can give and receive, where the sun rises and all is awash with freshness.

It was this finding of myself through ink, ink guided by that within, while having to believe very hard that there was something within. The ink formed a conduit, like blood in an arterial network and was critically important. That ink stared back at me and I knew that I existed.

> The light emanates
> from glass unshattered
> the wind blows
> through trees unblighted
> the body moves
> with infant ease
> and
> I implode as
> I feel the beauty.

> The light splits
> through crags unclimbed
> the bush exudes
> native tenderness
> and the ease and lushness
> touches unframed bodies
> to pass into
> the beauty of
> a world
> in need of
> nothing.

References

Andersen, T. (1987) The reflecting team: dialogue and meta-dialogue in clinical work, *Family Process*, 26(4): 415–28

Bakker, T. and Shuda, S. (1989) Distinctions, descriptions and explanations, in

J. Mason and J. Rubenstein (eds) *Family Therapy in South Africa Today*. Congella: South African Institute of Marital and Family Therapy.

Bateson, G. (1979) *Mind and Nature: A Necessary Unit*. New York: Bantam Books.

Bird, J. (2000) *The Heart's Narrative*. Auckland: Edge Press.

White, M. (1995) *Re-authoring Lives: Interviews and Essays*. Adelaide: Dulwich Centre Publications.

White, M. and Epston, D. (1990) *Narrative Means to Therapeutic Ends*. New York: Norton.

Chapter 8

Anticipating hope within written and naming domains of despair

Stephen Madigan

The anticipation of hope

Central to many psychotherapeutic services is the dual process of documenting client lives and relationships through naming and writing practices. How and what we identify and document is organized through set institutional, political and economic structures (Foucault 1965; Madigan 1996). Therapy – at least in theory – attempts to offer symptom relief and to bring forth 'positive' change. However, therapy and the structures that support these practices can sometimes weaken a person's ability to change and undermine any hope that change is possible (Gremillion 2003; Madigan 2003).

The idea of change, what constitutes change and what is considered change is under the direct influence of a therapy's conversational boundaries, linguistic territories, cultural structures and performance of theory. Therapeutic understanding, response and action is shaped by and shaping of these discursive parameters, offering discursive 'life' to both hopeful and despairing ideas (sometimes simultaneously) concerning the possibility of change.

This chapter addresses the process of production and reproduction in therapy while also offering a possible alternative to present and specific institutionalized naming and writing therapy practices. It also addresses the effect these processes have on the hope for change. I will attempt to show a method of addressing change through the therapeutic importance I place on the *anticipation* of hope, and I will demonstrate this through a case story, highlighting a variety of writing and naming practices used in my version of narrative therapy. These include the use of counter-viewing questions (Madigan 2003), therapeutic letter-writing campaigns (Madigan 1997, 1999), and the creation of communities of concern (Madigan and Epston 1995).

Naming and writing practices

Frustrated with therapy's 'rabid desire' to label 'things' and thereby sever these 'things' from their relational contexts, Gregory Bateson (1979) invited the field of family therapy to simply 'stamp out nouns'. He insisted that the 'thing' was not in fact the 'thing' named. Many family therapists found Bateson's idea interesting but quite difficult to achieve since our discursive practices of therapy name, and have a history of naming, central to the craft (Foucault 1965). Our educational, training and institutional settings encourage the establishment of set developmental 'norms' and meanings given to the naming of a 'client', 'woman', 'employee', 'father', 'child' and so on.

The field went further, giving fixed identities to persons and their experience, such as 'depressed client', ' anorexic woman', 'unruly employee', ' deadbeat father' and 'ADHD child'. Supplementary knowledge connected to the inscription of meaning also included cultural naming practices that marginalized and divided groups off from a 'mainstream' community of privileged others (see Madigan on Foucault 1992, 2003) such as 'single-parent client', 'native woman', 'gay employee', 'black inner-city male', 'South Asian immigrant', 'migrant worker', 'working-class father'. Names of this kind were negotiated, distributed, and meanings were accepted and documented – on some level by all our helping institutions.

The process of classifying persons and writing their histories into historical documents (files), through the template of 'soft' scientific research and investigation, acted to reproduce set cultural and institutional norms (Foucault 1973; Spivak 1996; Parker 1999). Helping professionals, finding themselves with an authority position to name 'others', were naming (labeling) from within pre-established institutional and cultural naming systems. What was reproduced within the name given was not only a newly inscribed identity politic but a verification (perhaps a valorization) that uplifted the legitimacy of scientific research and the status of the profession itself.

Within a name (for example, Obsessive Compulsive Disorder or Borderline), one's body is 'naturally' inscribed by rigorous science and the privileged status given to the naming and writing context (Grieves 1998; Gremillion 2003). Unfortunately, the everyday act of professional naming and writing persons', and groups of persons', bodies into categories, is often a finalized, decontextualized and pathologizing view of who they are and who they might become. The client is instructed to anticipate the limits of their life course in a particular and non-hopeful way.

Deciphering the person/problem named is usually a matter of interpreting and categorizing a 'cause' to explain the presenting problem. The cause (more often than not) is located and privatized within the person's abnormal body and genetically linked to other members of their family unit and their abnormal body(s). To uphold and support these modernist explanations for the cause of the problem, popular technologies of psychology (with the assistance of medicine, law, education, etc.) invented *interpretation* manuals to help decipher, name and locate symptoms. At the present time, there are over 400 possible ways to be named psychologically abnormal (Caplan 1995). This affords the pathology-oriented professional numerous ways to plot a client's life story with the help of the professional 'naming book', the *Diagnostic and Statistical Manual IV* (DSM-IV).

Within the model of scientific naming and writing, the body of the subject/client (you and me) is viewed as the passive tablet on which disordered names are written. Entering a helping system like a psychiatric hospital, a child care centre or a therapy clinic, the client is often required, due to insurance company claims and third party billing, to accept a disordered name before therapy can proceed. The name is further secured by the naming performance when 'it' is entered into professional filing sites (Foucault 1979) – for example, insurance, education, medical, judicial or employee. The history of our life file is cumulative and sometimes lasts forever (see also Chapter 7).

Naming: the cancelling out of hope

Professional stories written and told about the person – to the person prescribed and to others – maintain the powerfully pathologized plot, rhetorically embed the problem name (and personal life), and assist in piecing together states of despair. For the person looking for help and change, the naming and writing process of therapy used in North America can be both confusing and traumatic. Their answer to hope and possibility is to undergo further practices of therapeutic technology deemed hopeful and in concert with the practices of help offered to them by the very institution that named them. If they fail to change within the therapeutic parameters prescribed, the body will be further named. In this situation, the word 'chronic' is the name most often used – however, 'resistant' and 'unruly' are also not uncommon. This scenario presents a very difficult dilemma for clients. On the one hand they are named as chronic (no possibility for change) while on the other hand they are encouraged to change and blamed for not changing.

Perhaps the saddest flaw of this system of production is having to witness the full-on, heavy-handed negative effect that a professional's technology, skill and power has on the person's anticipation of change. What is supported in the life of the client is a community acceptance of despair and a 'cancelling out' of hope.

Discursive identity

Identities and our remembrances of our identities are profoundly political both in their origins and in their implications (Madigan 1996). Our distributed and negotiated selves (Tomm 1995) and the selves we normally remember are influenced by *and* reproductive of cultural and institutional norms. As contributing members of this community of identity and discourse, we come to experience ourselves within the relational politics of these dominant norms (are we normal, do we measure up, are we an acceptable and worthy citizen?).

'Identity', says feminist Jill Johnston, is 'what you can say you are, according to what they say you can be' (in Foucault 1989: 47). The identity she is referring to is *not* a freely created product of introspection or the unproblematic reflection of a private inner self (Spivak 1996). Identities are conceived within certain dialogic ideological frameworks constructed by the dominant social order to maintain its interests. Poststructuralists argue for a consideration of a post-humanist and decentralized view of persons (Hoagwood 1994; Butler 1997). This position unsettles any essentialist psychological notions of the stable autonomous person, the original author (of problem conversations or otherwise), or a given reality of what constitutes the self.

As far back as the early 1930s, the Russian linguist and psychologist Mikhail Bakhtin (1986) suggested that we are contributors to each other's identity. He wrote that 'I get a self that I can see, that I can understand and use, by clothing my otherwise invisible self in the completing categories I appropriate from the other's image of me' (p. 18). Bakhtin's view incorporates how the other plays a central role in constituting the individual self, and suggests that without the ongoing relationship to the other our 'selves' would be 'invisible, incomprehensible, and unusable' (p. 18). From this perspective, problems that persons encounter can be situated within a dialogic context and *not* placed under individual sovereignty. I would add that the professional viewpoint of clients or patients has been nurtured and influenced within the reigning dominant ideology of their profession and as such is considered immanent in the fields of worthy opinion and power relations.

A few narrative therapy understandings

In my view, narrative therapy attempts to demonstrate the poststructural dialogic view of the self, by highlighting and undermining dominant practices which act to specify, classify and subjugate a person's identity as fixed. This is so that counterclaims and documentation of resistance can be made. In addition, there are attempts made by the narrative therapist to render the status of identity-based politics transparent in the life of the problem, to map the influence these discursive practices have had on the person's life and to bring forth how they and others have resisted and responded outside the realm of the negative story being told (Wade 1997; Madigan and Law 1998).

To the narrative therapist, an identity is not viewed as fossilized within a problem. A person's identity is viewed within the politics and power plays of a manufactured and constituted self as discourse is produced (White and Epston 1990; Shotter 1991; Madigan 1996; Spivak 1996; Madigan and Law 1998). A narrative therapist's responsibility, then, lies in the question of which psychological and political orientations our practice ethics and therapeutic performance belong to.

Problems, identities and what information a person perceives and remembers are constitutive of lives and relationships (Foucault 1971; White 1991).

Persons and problems are constructed through an intricate dialogic inter-change of power and community discourses and reproduced within insti-tutions, families and relationships (Madigan 1996). As an initial step, practitioners introducing narrative ideas into therapy perceive that change occurs through recognizing and locating persons, practices, memories and problems within the dominant norms of the social domain.

Of central importance to those who practice narrative therapy is the bring-ing forth of re-remembered 'alternative' selves (some might say forgotten or unrecognized selves) and tracking alternative actions/thoughts/responses these selves took outside the realm of a specified problem identity. The spoken and written problem identity is not considered a fixed 'state', nor is it located within the person. The problem identity is viewed within the relational and political context of intricate negotiations that take place inside complex fields of power and discourse.

The consequence of an ideologically biased commerce of problems regu-larly finds a person's constructed identity very misrepresented and under-known by dominant knowledge and sets of agreed-upon thin conclusions (White 1992). Both the process of spoken and written pathologizing, and the technologies imported to implement the discourse of pathology, speak vol-umes about the dominant signifying mental health culture, but little of the person being pathologized.

For me, the narrative interview takes a therapeutic position to counter-view taken-for-granted ideas about problems, relationships and personhood (Madigan 2003), to rewrite the written (Madigan 1991), to re-remember and remember (Meyerhoff 1982; Madigan 1996, 1999; McCarthy 1999). As such a narrative therapeutic interview may be shaped by the following practices:

- Questions about how the 'known' and remembered problem identity of a person has been manufactured over time.
- Questions about what aspects of the social order have assisted in the ongoing maintenance of this remembered problem self.
- Locating those cultural apparatuses that keep this remembered problem self restrained from remembering alternative accounts and experiences of lived experience.
- Locating sites of resistance through questioning how the person can begin to re-remember alternative identities of self that live outside the cultural, professional and problem's version of them.
- Influencing how discursive space can give room for the possibilities of different kinds of discursive practices to emerge, by resisting and standing up for the performance of this re-remembered and preferred self.
- Exploring and finding out who else in the person's life might be engaged to offer accounts of re-remembrance and providing the person safety in membership.

Counter-viewing and narrative interviewing

In brief, I came up with the counter-viewing idea in 2001 after a lengthy watching of my therapy on video and realizing that much of the work involved 'raising suspicions' regarding the modernist/humanist accounts of the problem story being told, looking for contradictions that could not be readily accounted for within the story, being curious as to how people could account for these differences, and appreciating and acknowledging these acts of cultural resistance. This method of 'close up' interviewing and relating to others engages the relational world of therapeutic interviewing in the following way. Counter-viewing:

- is an intensely critical mode of reading professional systems of meaning and *unravelling* the ways these systems work to dominate and name;
- views all written professional texts (files) about the client as ways to lure the therapist into taking certain ideas about the person for granted and into privileging certain ways of knowing and being over others;
- is an unravelling of professional and cultural works through a kind of anti-method which resists a prescription. It is looking for how a problem is produced and reproduced rather than wanting to pin it down and say this is really what it is;
- looks for ways in which our understanding and room for movement is limited by the lines of persuasion operating in discourse;
- leads us to explore the ways in which our own therapeutic understanding of problems is located in discourse;
- allows us to reflect on how we make and remake our lives through moral-political projects embedded in a sense of justice rather than a given psychiatric diagnosis.

Counter-viewing and narrative therapy – the issue of respect

Counter-viewing in therapy is profoundly respectful as it attempts to do justice to the stories people tell about their distress, respect the experience they have with the problems of living, appreciate the struggles they are embarking on, and appreciate and document how they have responded to the problem. The task is to work within these descriptions and acknowledge the complexity of the story being told so that contradictions can be opened up and used to bring forth something different by sustained reflection towards a sparkling undergrowth needing attention. Noting the contradictions allows for the elaboration of competing perspectives as the person's story unravels. These different competing perspectives seem to lie side-by-side and fit together but there is a tension between them as they seem to try and make us see the world in different ways at one and the same time.

A one-perspective story holds the person in the grip of the problem's/ professionals' point of view. And against this professional standpoint there is the perspective that flows from the client who is simultaneously trying to find ways of shaking the problem and perhaps escaping the branded name altogether. To be respectful to the differing viewpoints does not mean abandoning our own standpoint, but it does mean acknowledging where we stand.

Counter-viewing and narrative therapy – the issue of critique

Counter-viewing in therapy is intensely critical of many therapy practices which are embedded in images of the self and others, that systematically mislead us as to the 'nature' of problems. It does this in not presupposing a self which lies 'under the surface' as it were. Counter-viewing also alerts us to the ways that dominant ideas of the self get smuggled into therapy under the disguise of 'helping' others.

Dominant narratives of mental distress can all too quickly lock us back into the problem at the very moment we think we have found a way out. The task of counter-viewing therapists and counter-viewing clients is to locate problems in cultural practices in order to comprehend the role of patterns of power that give people the idea that they alone are to blame for these problems, they are helpless to do anything about these problems and they should not maintain much hope. In counter-viewing practices, change is seen to occur when we are working collaboratively through the spaces of resistance opened up and made available by the competing accounts and alternative practices. It is here that hope can rise again.

Therapeutic letter-writing campaign

I came up with the idea of the therapeutic letter-writing campaign after many long discussions, since 1991, with my friends, narrative therapists David Epston and Michael White. It was at this time I had the good fortune to live and work alongside them in New Zealand and Australia during my time on a family therapy scholarship they had awarded me. The letter campaign idea was also influenced through the occasion of my mother's surprisingly early and sudden death in the late fall of 1992. In brief, my immigrant Irish parents raised my two sisters and me in a working-class neighbourhood of Toronto, Canada, where it seemed like our entire community was made up of an Irish Catholic diaspora. Along with the tradition of sending Mass cards at the time of the death, a few of her lifelong friends penned letters of love outlining the profound importance my mother had played in their daily lives. The power of their written rememberances had an enormously helpful and hopeful effect on my family. A year or two later, I began running anti-anorexic and multiple family groups two days a week at an eating disorder (ED) unit through a hospital in Vancouver, Canada.

Merging all three experiences together – studying with David and Michael, my mother's friends' letters, and the ED unit – I created the practice of therapeutic letter-writing campaigns in response to the deadly effects the culture of anorexia and bulimia was having on the lives and relationships of the people I was encountering on the ED ward.

Statistically, persons diagnosed with anorexia and/or bulimia experience the highest death rate of any 'mental illness' in North America (Madigan and Goldner 1999). The people struggling are believed by the mental health profession to be 'very difficult' clients to treat, have pounds of pathologized papered files written about them, are given multiple diagnoses (borderline, depressed, and obsessive compulsive disorder are the most common), are subsequently medicated to the gills and are often told – overtly and covertly – that they have very little chance of 'recovery'. My letter campaign was a structured attempt to create a *community of concern* (Madigan and Epston 1995) to help break with the despairing view of the person suffering and to assist in the re-remembering of unique aspects of their lives now restrained by cultural, professional and problem discourses. In short, the campaign was designed to bring forth the anticipation of hope and the possibility of a healthy life.

The logic behind the community letter-writing campaign was also an attempt at finding ways to respond to the problem identity growing stronger within the structures of the institution (see Gremillion 2003; Madigan and Goldner 1999). There appeared to be a correlation between the person being cut off from hope and forgotten experiences of themselves and relationships that lived outside of their 'sick' identity, and the rapidly growing professional file of hopelessness. The thought was to counterbalance the issue by including a community of remembering and loving others who held the stories of the client. These were stories that lived outside the professional and cultural inscription that defined the person suffering. They were also stories that stood on the belief that change was possible.

Together with the client I would write a letter to selected members of family and friends (and other clients on and off the ward whom they knew), and ask them to assist in a temporal re-remembering and witnessing process through lettered written accounts outlining their (a) memories of their relationship with the client, (b) their current hopes for the client and (c) how they anticipated their relationship growing with the client in the future. These written accounts were directed squarely at countering the problem strategies. They were diametrically different from what had been written in the client file. They represented a *counter file*. Documenting alternative versions counteracted the infirming effects of the professional and cultural problem story, and the pathologized names inscribed on their bodies.

I have found that these lettered accounts hold a tremendous potential for highlighting sites of resistance and performed a re-storying of persons' lives and relationships (Madigan 1999). After utilizing these strategies on the

ED ward, I then began to use therapeutic letter-writing campaigns, counter-viewing and creating communities of concern in a variety of other despairing problem situations.

Peter's story

The social work department of an inpatient adult psychiatric ward asked if I would 'see' Peter, a 38-year-old white, heterosexual, married middle-class man. This particular psychiatric ward often refers their patients and families to me, and it seemed from the social worker's point of view that Peter and I were potentially a good therapeutic match.

Peter was described to me by hospital professionals as 'chronically depressed' and was given very little hope for change. The pessimism was triggered as a result of recent attempts to kill himself while on the ward and having to be physically restrained for pushing a male orderly. The hospital's plan for health and change involved group and individual cognitive behavioral therapy together with numerous medications. Despite these attempts, the hospital said to me that 'nothing seemed to be working'. I was also informed that the staff were beginning to think that after six months' ward time 'change was impossible'.

Peter had a total of eight visits with me over the course of five months. After the first six meetings he was able to return home from the hospital. All therapy sessions included a reflecting team (Madigan 1991). On five of the visits, volunteers on the letter-writing campaign (including family members, long-time friends and his former partner, Caitland, from whom he had separated) were invited into therapy to 'perform' their written work 'live' in front of Peter.

The 'general' structure for reading and witnessing the letters in therapy is as follows:

1 All campaign writers are invited to the session (if this is geographically possible) and in turn are asked to read aloud the letter they had penned about the 'patient'. In this case it was in front of Peter, me, the other writers of his community and the team.
2 After each writer reads aloud, the client is asked to read the letter back to the writer, so both writer and client can attend to what is being said/written from the different positions of speaking and listening.
3 After each letter is read by the writer and discussed with the client, the

community of others in the session (who are sitting and listening) offer a brief reflection of what the letter evoked in their own personal lives.

4   This process continues until all letters are read, re-read, responded to and reflected upon.

5   Each reflecting team member (usually made up of professionals) then writes and reads a short letter to the client and their community. They reflect on the counter-view of the client offered up by them and their community, the hope that was shared and aspects of the letters that moved them personally.

6   Copies are made of each letter and given to everyone in attendance.

7   I then follow up the session with a therapeutic letter addressed to everyone who attended, including the client, the community and the reflecting team. In Peter's case, letters were also forwarded to the hospital team.

> During the first interview, Peter explained that 11 months prior to our talk, his 3-year-old daughter (whose mother was his former partner Caitland) had died in a tragic swimming accident. He stated that initially he had only felt 'bitter and angry', and 'cut off' from the 'real meaning to life' and 'turned down support from anyone that mattered'. He stated that he responded by 'barricading myself away from the world; I blamed myself', and shortly thereafter separating from Caitland 'to be alone'. Peter had virtually removed himself from anyone who cared about him. He was eventually admitted to the ward after a neighbour 'by the grace of God' found him 'in the garage with the motor running'.
>
> The problem, which he referred to as 'an inability to go on', had taken over his daily life. He let us know that he was 'haunted day and night' and 'couldn't remember much of his life' from before the day his daughter Mara died. He said that he 'felt hopeless' and could not remember the 'sound of Mara's voice'.

Briefly, I have outlined below some of the therapeutic counter-viewing questions that Peter and I engaged in:

•   Do you think a 'giving up on hope' is the way in which your conversations with hopelessness find a way to help you believe that 'giving up' is a good answer – the only answer?

•   How do you think the community looks on a father who has lost his 3-year-old daughter?

•   Do you think it is fair that everyone keeps telling you to 'get over it'?

- Do you believe that these people believe that there is a proper timeline for a grieving father?
- Are there places of past hope that you can remember that are currently blocked out by hopelessness and despair?
- How is this hope possible?
- Do you find any hope in the fact that Dave, your neighbour, pulled you out of the garage before death took you?
- Do you feel that it is a fair accusation to blame yourself for Mara's death?
- Was the hospital accurate in diagnosing you as depressed or do you think it might be about your experience of not knowing 'how to go on'?
- Why do you think the hospital gave a grieving father so much medication?
- Are there people in your life, including the hospital staff, that you believe blame you for Mara's death?
- Has this deep sorrow you've explained to me been a sorrow that you could share with anyone else?
- Is there any one person or any one idea that promotes a life of hopelessness within your day-to-day living?
- Is there anyone in your life, looking in on your life, that you think holds out hope for you by holding your hope for you until you return to it?
- If for a moment you could imagine that hope could be rediscovered in your life, what present qualities in you would give it staying power?
- Was there ever a time that you disputed your internal conversations of blame and hopelessness?
- Is the love you hold for Mara in any way helpful to the restoration of hope in your life?

After three sessions Peter, the team and I drafted a letter to his community of concern. He chose a dozen people to mail the letter out to. The letter read:

Dear friends and family of Peter

My name is Stephen Madigan and I am a family therapist working alongside Peter. Since Mara's tragic death Peter has let me know that 'he hasn't known how to face the world'. Up until recently a sense of 'hopelessness' has pretty much taken over his life, to the point that it almost killed him. Another debilitating aspect of this profound loss is that Peter can't 'remember much of his life' since before Mara's death. Peter also feels in an 'odd way responsible for Mara's death', even though he knows 'somewhere in his mind' that he 'was out of town the day of the accident'. Peter believes that there is a 'strong message out there' that he 'should just get on with his life'. Peter says he finds this attitude 'troubling' because each 'person is different' and he believes that he 'might never get over it but eventually learn to live with it'.

We are writing to ask you to write a letter in support of Peter explaining (a) memories of your life with Peter, (b) what you shared, (c) who Mara was to you, (d) how you plan to support Peter while he grieves, (e) what Peter has given to you in your life and (f) what you think your lives will be like together once he leaves the hospital.

Thank you for your help,

Peter, Stephen and the team

I personally found the reflections and readings with Peter, and the eight members of his community who attended, extremely profound. Our letter-writing campaign meetings sometimes lasted two or three hours (we schedule them at day's end). There is not space in this chapter to include the campaign and reflection letters sent and read, but suffice to say that the texts written by the community of concern acted upon Peter's anticipation of hope and his willingness to further live his life.

Four weeks after Peter left the hospital, free of medication and concern, he and Mara's mother Caitland entered into therapy with me to try and restore their marriage. They brought the letters. They anticipated the possibility that they could reconstruct their marriage. Hope is a wonderful potion.

References

Bakhtin, M.M. (1986) *Speech Genres and Other Late Essays*, trans. Vern McGee. Austin, TX: University of Texas Press.

Bateson, G. (1979) *Mind and Nature: A Necessary Unity*. New York: Bantam Books.

Butler, J. (1997) *Excitable Speech: A Politics of the Performance*. New York: Routledge.

Caplan, P. (1995) *They Say You're Crazy: How the World's Most Powerful Psychiatrists Decide Who's Normal*. New York: Addison-Wesley Publishing.

Foucault, M. (1965) *Madness and Civilization: A History of Insanity in the Age of Reason*. New York: Random House.

Foucault, M. (1971) Nietzche, genealogy, history, in D. Bouchard (ed.) *Language, Counter-Memory, Practice: Selected Essays and Interviews*. Ithaca: Cornell University Press, 1977.

Foucault, M. (1973) *The Birth of the Clinic: An Archeology of Medical Perception*. London: Tavistock Publications.

Foucault, M. (1979) *Discipline and Punish: The Birth of the Prison*. Harmondsworth: Penguin.

Foucault, M. (1989) *Foucault Live: Collected Interviews, 1961–1984*, ed. S. Lotringer. New York: Semiotext(e).

Gremillion, H. (2003) *Feeding Anorexia: Gender and Power at a Treatment Centre*. Durham, CA: Duke University Press.

Grieves, L. (1998) From beginning to start: the Vancouver anti-anorexia/anti-bulimia league, in S. Madigan and I. Law (eds) *PRAXIS: Situating Discourse, Feminism and Politics in Narrative Therapies*. Vancouver: Yaletown Family Therapy Press.

Hoagwood, K. (1994) Poststructuralist historism and the psychological construction of anxiety disorders, *The Journal of Psychology*, 127(1): 105–22.

Law, I. and Madigan, S. (1994) Power and politics in practice, in I. Law and S. Madigan (eds) *Dulwich Newsletter*, special edition, 3: 8.

McCarthy, I. (1999) Personal communication, Dublin, Ireland.

Madigan, S. (1991) Discursive restraints in therapist practice: reflecting and listening, *Dulwich Centre Newsletter*, 3: 13–20.

Madigan, S. (1992) The application of Michel Foucault's philosophy in the problem externalizing discourse of Michael White, *Journal of Family Therapy*, 14(3): 19–37.

Madigan, S. (1996) The politics of identity: considering community discourse in the externalising of internalised discourse, *Journal of Systemic Therapy*, 10(1): 47–63.

Madigan, S. (1997) Re-considering memory: rerembering lost identities back towards re-membered selves, in D. Nylund and C. Smith (eds) *Narrative Therapy with Children*. New York: Guilford.

Madigan, S. (1999) Destabilizing chronic identities of depression and retirement, in I. Parker (ed.) *Deconstructing Psychotherapy*. London: Sage.

Madigan, S. (2003) Injurious speech: counterviewing eight conversational habits of highly effective problems, *International Journal of Narrative Therapy and Community Work*, 2(1): 43–60.

Madigan, S. and Epston, D. (1995) From spy-chiatric gaze to communities of concern: from professional monologue to dialogue, in S. Friedman (ed.) *The Reflecting Team in Action*. New York: Guilford.

Madigan, S. and Goldner, E. (1999) A narrative approach to anorexia: discourse, reflexivity and questions, in M. Hoyt (ed.) *Constructive Therapies*. New York: Guilford.

Madigan, S. and Law, I. (eds) (1998) *PRAXIS: Situating Discourse, Feminism and Politics in Narrative Therapies*. Vancouver: Yaletown Family Therapy Press.

Myerhoff, B. (1982) Life history among the elderly: performance, visibility and remembering, in J. Ruby (ed.) *Crack in the Mirror: Reflexive Perspectives in Anthropology*. Philadelphia, PA: University of Pennsylvania Press.

Parker, I. (1999) *Social Construction, Discourse and Realism*. London: Sage.

Shotter, J. (1991) Personal communication, NOVA Southeastern University, Fort Lauderdale, FL.

Spivak, G. (1996) Diaspora old and new: women in the transnational world, *Textual Practice*, 10(2): 245–69

Tomm, K. (1995) Personal communciation, Vancouver, Canada.

Wade, A. (1997) Small acts of living: everyday resistance to violence and other forms of oppression, *Contemporary Family Therapy*, 19(1): 23–40.

White, M. (1991) Personal communication, Adelaide, Australia.

White, M. (1992) Personal communication, Adelaide, Australia.

White, M. and Epston, D. (1990) *Narrative Means to Therapeutic Ends*. New York: Norton.

Chapter 9

Hope in the process: conducting systemically orientated trauma work within the context of the peace process in Northern Ireland

Stephen Coulter, Arlene Healey and Isobel Reilly

Introduction

Beginning with a brief summary of the historical context of the conflict in Northern Ireland which will help readers situate our practice, this chapter develops the themes of hope and despair within two separate but connected frames – the sociopolitical and the therapeutic. Using case vignettes we consider how the peace process has affected the therapeutic process and the crossover between the two domains. Within our approach to trauma recovery we describe how we attempt to counter the pull of despair the work can generate, alongside balancing the sensitivity and attention paid to external processes over which we can seem helpless.

The conflict and the peace process

For the past 36 years Northern Ireland has been a society engaged in a civil conflict, widely referred to as the Troubles. There have been more than 3700 people killed (McKittrick *et al.* 1999) and 47,500 people seriously injured (PSNI 2003). These figures are significant in a population of 1.6 million.

The conflict is a complex sectarian dispute characterized by violence perpetrated between two communities, one of broadly Roman Catholic/Nationalist identity (with ideological allegiance to a united Ireland) and the other of broadly Protestant/Unionist identity (ideologically allied to the continuing union with Britain). The legitimacy of Northern Ireland as part of the United Kingdom has been at the heart of the conflict. Republican paramilitary groups such as the Irish Republican Army (IRA) describe themselves as waging a 'war' on the 'occupying' British forces while those in the security forces see themselves upholding the rule of law against a terrorist threat.

For many years stoicism and silence were the preferred ways of coping with the human psychological cost of the Troubles (McCormick 1997; Campbell and Healey 1999; Fay *et al.* 1999). Kapur (2001: 267) writes, 'Northern

Ireland society as a large group has, until recently, remained in the distress and denial phase of the troubles and is only now beginning to wake up to the level of destruction it has inflicted on itself.'

A tentative peace process begun in the early 1990s led to ceasefire declarations by several key paramilitary groups in 1994. After extensive multi-party negotiations the Belfast Agreement (Office of the First Minister and Deputy First Minister (OFMDFM) 1998) set out a way forward to power-sharing through a locally elected assembly. The Agreement addressed difficult issues including: the constitutional status of Northern Ireland; early release of paramilitary prisoners; renaming and restructuring the police service; demilitarization and reduction of British Army presence; and the decommissioning of paramilitary weapons.

The Belfast Agreement is a complex settlement, built on a 'win–win' premise that sought 'a balance of pain' for both communities as the price to be paid for the prize of sustainable peace. Initial optimism, including a period in which the new devolved legislative assembly operated relatively successfully, gradually dissipated under the weight of lack of progress on implementing key aspects of the Agreement. The outcome was a breakdown of workable relations between the major political parties and a retreat into mistrust and suspicion.

Our therapeutic context – the Family Trauma Centre

The authors are all employed as systemic family therapists at the Family Trauma Centre in Belfast. The Centre was established by the government in 1999 with the specific remit of addressing the therapeutic needs of children, young people and their families who are suffering psychological trauma related to the conflict in Northern Ireland.

The Family Trauma Centre has worked to create an environment that is welcoming and a place in which those who attend can feel safe to tell their stories (Healey 2004). This is not a simple task given that clients come from all the parties to the conflict and many have issues of safety and trust. The relatively small population and traditionally strong family and community connections in Northern Ireland can compound this difficulty. For instance, appointment scheduling comes into sharp focus when we are seeing both parties to a particular incident.

Creating safety is therefore a critical initial phase of the therapeutic process (Coulter 2001). It may involve discussion with potential clients about where best to be seen, for example home visit, outreach clinic, the Centre itself. It also includes openness about how records are kept and the limits of confidentiality when issues of serious risk arise. Profound helplessness and unpredictability are at the heart of the traumatic experience (Herman 1992; American Psychiatric Association 1994). We endeavour to afford a high degree of control regarding the timing, methods and pacing of the therapeutic work, coupled with predictability in terms of place, staff and therapeutic environment. Thus we seek to avoid unwittingly mirroring the dynamics of the traumatic experience.

Given our Troubles-related remit, there is potential for the political to become included in the therapeutic process. Our context is one in which it is all too easy to identify one's community and ethnic identity by such simple things as first and surnames, pronunciation of certain words, engagement in certain cultural and sporting activities and the language we use about government and the conflict. There are many situations in which acknowledgement of the therapists' and clients' identities are important to create an open working space for the therapy to take place. We are open about our therapeutic teams being drawn from both main traditions in Northern Ireland. We are also fortunate to have colleagues from outside Northern Ireland, bringing a more 'not knowing' perspective to our engagement with difference.

Through these counter-trauma processes we provide a therapeutic space in which all stories brought to the Centre can be told and witnessed. Gratifyingly, we have repeatedly found that in this atmosphere subjugated and marginalized accounts begin to emerge, empowering previously untold stories to be given voice (Weingarten 2003).

Shifting sands – the peace process as an ever-changing context

Over the period in which this chapter has been written our thoughts about hope and despair in our particular context have been directly affected by the hurtling highs and lows of the roller-coaster that is the Northern Ireland peace process. In the space of nine months there have been periods of stalling, inertia and standoff along with flurries of negotiations, formal statements and promises of breakthroughs.

Representatives of the British and Irish governments and the two more extreme major parties (which in recent elections both eclipsed their more moderate rivals) were edging towards completing a deal that would finally see the full implementation of the Belfast Agreement. However, in the end the process foundered on the issue of photographic evidence of the decommissioning of IRA weapons and the prime ministers could only publish what would have been the elements of such a deal.[1]

The massive Northern Bank robbery on 20 December 2004 (widely believed to be perpetrated by the IRA) forced other parties to review Sinn Fein's[2] sincerity during the recent talks. The murder of Robert McCartney on 30 January 2005 and the determined search for justice by his partner and five sisters have further focused national and international attention on the contradiction of Sinn Fein's position in relation to the IRA in a way that the murder of 38 other people (allegedly) by the IRA in the last ten years had failed to do. These events were an almost fatal blow to the remnants of fragile trust and placed the peace process in cold storage. A recent statement from the IRA that the 'war' is over is again promoting hope in the process.

Hope and despair in the clinical work

The highs and lows of the peace process have been complicated by the fact that in a strongly sectarian society politics have been described as a zero sum game – i.e. if they are getting something we must be losing something. Thus one person's highs are often another person's lows. Through a series of case vignettes we explore how this context impacts on the therapeutic process, and the interplay of hope and despair in our clients, as well as in us as therapists, as society edges towards a 'shared future' (OFMDFM 2005).

No reprieve

Mr Wilson, a middle-aged man from the Protestant community, illustrates the impact of the provision for early release of political prisoners in the Belfast Agreement. Mr Wilson was the victim of two separate bombing incidents in the same locality, 21 years apart, the first occurring in 1972, the second in 1993, when the imperative for peace was well under way though the ceasefires of 1994 had yet to be reached. It is what happened subsequent to the second incident that illustrates the pull of despair and how it can all but negate the positive potential for hope.

> Mr Wilson and his son were walking past a fast food outlet on the Shankill Road in Belfast on Saturday 23 October 1993 on their way to support their local soccer team when a bomb exploded, killing ten people. They were among the 57 injured and spent several days in an intensive care unit. Mr Wilson sustained internal bruising, a serious laceration to his back and numerous small shrapnel wounds to his head and face. He had helped others in the immediate aftermath of the explosion. One of the perpetrators of the Shankill Road bomb was killed and another injured when the bomb detonated prematurely. Mr Wilson later realized that he had directed medical care to the surviving perpetrator after the explosion. The perpetrator was subsequently convicted and given nine life sentences and a 25-year sentence for causing an explosion.
>
> Mr Wilson made extensive use of individual trauma treatment at the Family Trauma Centre and his condition stabilized despite some minor lapses. However, when the bomber was released early on licence under the Belfast Agreement after serving only seven years of his sentence,

Mr Wilson experienced a significant setback. Pictures of the perpetrator smiling and greeted by friends were broadcast. Mr Wilson was distressed by these images and started drinking heavily. He felt despair in relation to the apparent fragility of his psychological recovery and also to feelings of injustice about the early release of prisoners. He echoed the views of many victims and their families when he said that there could never be any early release from their losses.

Recently Mr Wilson re-engaged with the Family Trauma Centre. This followed a loyalist paramilitary assault and intimidation in his home, including the threat of death. The paramilitaries were angry with him for criticizing their vengeful retaliation in response to the bomb, and repudiating the notion that they had killed Catholics on his behalf.

Betrayed

The second case example tracks over time the fluctuations in feelings of both hope and despair as set against the backdrop of the peace process.

The Evans family, father John (40) and mother Joan (39), and their two children Jonny (18) and Susan (14), live on the outskirts of Belfast. John had worked as a prison officer for the past 25 years and Joan was employed in the public sector. Jonny and Susan are still at school. The family were referred following a bomb attack to their home which caused serious damage. They had previously been attacked several months before when a brick was thrown through the living-room window. The sense of continuing threat to their safety resulted in the family moving house.

The whole family chose to attend and in the initial meeting their fears about coming to the Centre and concerns about safety and security were addressed. We were aware that in the recent past, and as one of the 'lows' in the peace process, records were stolen from a hospital in Belfast and as a result a number of prison officers whose names and addresses were included in these records were advised to relocate. Following open discussion of these experiences with the family the team agreed not to record their address and correspond with them via a relative.

The family described how for more than 20 years they had lived in fear of attack from republican paramilitary groups. John's daily experience involved checking his car for explosive devices, varying his routes to work and avoiding high-risk areas when off-duty. The children also led very vigilant lives, being careful whom they confided in and usually describing their father's occupation by the generic term 'civil servant'.

As the peace process got under way the threat from republican paramilitary groups substantially diminished. However, the hope of a more normal existence was soon extinguished by an increase in attacks on prison personnel by loyalist paramilitaries. This followed the re-arrest of several paramilitary leaders, despite their early release. The intimidation and the bomb attack the Evans family suffered felt like a betrayal as they share the same religious affiliation as the perpetrators. This was further compounded by the fact that John's employers and the police had failed to take the previous brick attack seriously, assessing the risk to the family as low. As a result nothing had been done to improve the family's security. Even after the bomb attack it was not John's employers who referred the family, but a local politician to whom they had turned for help and support.

The impact of this trauma had led to deterioration in Joan's physical health due to persistent stress and at times overwhelming feelings of hopelessness about the future. Jonny despairs of ever having a normal life after being involved in a violent incident at a party with some young people who had paramilitary connections. John feels his employers do not accept the seriousness of the psychological damage to him and his family as a result of these experiences. Understandably, he feels anger and powerlessness about the way he has been treated and this has added to the guilt he feels. At one point a medical practitioner suggested that he should go back to work to improve his health, resulting in John having suicidal thoughts and concerns about his sanity.

In addition to the recurrent theme of betrayal two other interconnected themes emerged in our conversations. One was the pervading sense of loss. The family lost their home of 25 years, the children felt they had lost their dad, and John thought he was not the father he should be. Joan gave up a job she loved to avoid people with paramilitary connections. The other theme has catalysed around their continuing sense of insecurity and threat, with its chronic effects on the day-to-day lives of all the family. Feeling unsupported by state agencies after a lifetime serving the state has compounded their despair. John in particular feels abandoned by those he served.

The therapeutic work included individual work for each family member and regular family sessions, primarily using the reflecting team approach (Andersen 1991). In the initial session the family's reactions to the team's reflections were striking. John and Joan both began to cry. They said that listening to the team had been a very moving experience, that they felt as 'though they had been given hundreds of pounds' because their story had been heard. Up until that point they said they often felt as if people thought they were exaggerating the impact that the attack had on their lives. This re-emphasized for us value of therapeutic witnessing and the difference this can make to a misunderstood and isolated family (Perlesz 1999). The family therapy sessions gave time and spaces for reflection, affording the opportunity to create a more rounded understanding of their difficulties as a family and achieve a greater appreciation of each other's responses and reactions.

Coherent meaning-making for the family has been compromised by the rapidly changing political context and the state's inadequate response to their situation. These factors have brought waves of both hope and despair to the family. However, in our most recent meeting with the family hope has emerged as the more dominant. The family directly attribute this greater sense of hope about the future to the conversations at the Family Trauma Centre and the work we have done together.

The dirty war

The peace process allowed a wider recognition of illegal acts by agents of the state during the Troubles. Inquiries into allegations of collusion in the murders of prominent solicitors Patrick Finucane and Rosemary Nelson, and of loyalist paramilitary leader William Wright while in prison, have been put on the agenda. A public inquiry into the killing of 13 unarmed civilians in (London) Derry on 'Bloody Sunday' in 1972 has recently completed hearing evidence from some 900 witnesses over more than four years and costing to date £155m.

In contrast there are many stories that have not received as much attention in the public arena. These stories are often recounted in the therapeutic domain. One such instance is that of a young man murdered by a loyalist gang. His family are haunted by the circumstances surrounding the shooting, believing the security forces complicit in the murder. They describe how only 30 minutes before the shooting, security force vehicles were seen in the area. The shooting took place in the afternoon and the perpetrators' car was not apprehended despite the immediate notification of the police. The family believe the security forces made sure it was safe for the killers to enter and leave the area. The family's frustration at their helplessness in the face of what appears to be state collusion hinders their adjustment to the loss. Whether any of the truth recovery processes being mooted as part of the peace process would reveal the information the family are seeking remains an open question.

Retaining hope in the process

The work described above illustrates how inevitably both the clinical process and its possible outcomes walk hand-in-hand with what is happening in the wider sociopolitical context. In respect of post-conflict transitional societies, Sluzki (2003) noted that beginning the process of transformation may be frustratingly slow and out of synch with the hopes and aspirations of the people. As described above, progress, setbacks and stalemate in the peace process can be reflected in the therapeutic encounter. Movement in terms of resolving emotional and psychological conflict at a personal level is connected to wider societal influences for many of our clients. The lack of consensus about the political settlement is felt at community and familial levels, and seeps into therapy.

Despite all its difficulties the peace process has brought a marked decrease in sectarian killing. The historical sectarian dispute now tends to be re-enacted in various forms at 'interfaces' in Belfast at times of heightened tension involving violent attacks on the other community. An interface is the geographic area close to a 'peace line' or 'peace wall'. These are walls built several metres high, separating opposing sides of the conflict. Incursions into 'enemy' territory are responded to with retaliation.

In 2001 the Protestant residents of Glenbryn caught the attention of world media by attempting to stop pupils attending Holy Cross Girls' Primary School. The protesters perceived their area being systematically taken over by people from the neighbouring Catholic area. Families from both sides of the dispute were referred to the Family Trauma Centre: we saw children directly traumatized by running the gauntlet of angry adults shouting abuse; and children who had been traumatized by the police in full riot gear clearing protesters off the street and searching homes. In parallel with our direct clinical work (Reilly et al. 2004) we consulted schools and community groups and thus began to encompass a wider community dimension in the work. This is a good fit with our relational perspective on trauma recovery (Landau and Saul 2004) where we position individual trauma symptom reduction alongside family sessions and community outreach.

There is hope that this interface activity may be losing its impetus. Trouble at interfaces tends to be sparked by local issues or incidents rather than by the wider political picture. The heart seems to have gone out of the fight and there appears to be no stomach for a return to widespread community conflict. Our firm hope is that the will of the people for peace is now so strong that a renewed campaign of sectarian violence (from whatever quarter) would not be sustainable.

Alongside this hope sits a growing despair at the rise in intra-community violence as paramilitary groups seek to consolidate and extend their hold on communities. In 2000 a bitter internal feud broke out among loyalist paramilitary groups, with many families affected by several weeks of intimidation including bullets delivered through the mail, paint thrown over family cars and windows smashed. As tension rose, more direct action occurred, usually under cover of darkness. Homes were bombed and arson attacks made, resulting in a number of families being forced to abandon their homes. These incidents had a profound impact on families' sense of safety. One child slept with a kitchen knife under his pillow. A teenager tied a knife to a large stick and kept it by his bed. Parents were constantly checking locks and doors and reported taking turns 'on watch', looking out for signs of impending trouble.

'Own group' violence can also take the form of community-based 'policing' (Jarman 2004). A particular feature of this is the brutal punishment meted out to young people who have transgressed: for example, stealing cars for 'joy riding' and other petty crime. While circumscribed by locality, the effects have been witnessed by the population as a whole as rarely a day goes by without our being reminded through media reporting of the latest act of vigilante justice. The punishments involve extreme acts of violence by groups of men on the alleged perpetrators and have long-term consequences, both physical and psychological.

Personal, professional and political perspectives on hope and despair

Our staff group is mindful of the societal and political contexts within which we work. However, it is not only in the domain of work that connections are made. We too have been exposed to a (more or less) sectarian upbringing and have stories to tell and experiences to recount. Memories, perhaps largely forgotten, are ready to be reawakened by the right trigger.

Issues of risk and safety have played a central part in our shared experiences of living as part of a divided community, where what you are perceived to be by way of religious identity is often much more important than how you might wish to describe yourself. We all share memories of, at the very least, safety checks and roadblocks, detours to avoid contentious flash points and community confrontations. Some staff have been directly affected by the impact of traumatic events and all have been exposed through media coverage. As therapists we could define our witnessing position as aware but unempowered (Weingarten 2000, 2003).

Hope and despair coexist (Perlesz 1999) and are not inversely proportional. Currently for us hope and despair seem to run along parallel, connected tracks that may relate to different time frames. We may despair in the short term of the failure of our politicians to follow through on the Belfast Agreement and of the recent obvious breaches of trust. Without locally accountable government actively working towards a rights-based society there seems little hope of paramilitary control being lessened and the number of new victims being significantly reduced.

At the same time we are fundamentally hopeful that the earlier justifications for the conflict have been effectively removed by the British and Irish governments through structural reforms and changes in their official stances about sovereignty, thus negating the purpose of politically motivated violence. We are also hopeful that our communities have already moved so far in the direction of relative peace that any attempt to return to widespread conflict would not be supported. 'The deal' must inevitably be done, though perhaps later rather than sooner. Recent events may influence international opinion and give families encouragement to resist the malign effects of paramilitary control. Our clients might then begin to benefit from a 'peace dividend'.

Drawing on the theory of coordinated management of meaning (Cronen and Pearce 1982; Cronen et al. 1982) it is increasingly apparent, and hopeful, that *implicative forces* are being harnessed to counter the weight of the oppressive sociocultural forces in which sectarianism is embedded. News of difference is getting out and about, opportunities for increasingly different dialogue (Pearce and Pearce 1998) between community grassroots groups are developing with an unstoppable and generative dynamism that competes more or less on an equal footing with the pervasive pessimism we have been used to.

The Belfast Agreement relied on there being a 'balance of pain' for the two main communities in order for society to move forwards. It is often those who have suffered most who are asked to absorb the most pain. Victims have been valiantly struggling with the question, 'Is the pain we are being asked to accept worth it for a political settlement?' Despite recent developments this question remains premature.

Conclusion

In Northern Ireland the weight of the contextual forces operating at the sociopolitical level inevitably choreographs our interactions and dealings with each other, in whatever domain – personal or professional. At times we feel in a state of 'truce or freeze' (Sluzki 2003), and the lack of progress in the peace process places us all in an unstable vacuum. The phase we are currently in is one of coexistence (Chayes and Minow 2003). Alongside the vying for power at the political level as the peace process continues its faltering way, the question for us as therapists in our particular setting, is how best we can progress in our work, 'doing hope' (Weingarten 2003) and countering the pull of despair. This is our continuing endeavour.

Notes

1 Loyalist paramilitary groups continue to be active on the ground but have been largely sidelined in the political process due to lack of a significant electoral mandate.
2 Sinn Fein are widely believed to be the political representatives of the IRA.

References

American Psychiatric Association (1994) *Diagnostic and Statistical Manual of Mental Disorders*, 4th edn. Washington, DC: APA.

Andersen, T. (ed.) (1991) *The Reflecting Team: Dialogues and Dialogues about Dialogues.* New York: Norton.

Campbell, J. and Healey, A. (1999) Whatever you say, say something: the education, training and practice of mental health social workers in Northern Ireland, *Social Work Education*, 18(4): 389–400.

Chayes, A. and Minow M. (eds) (2003) *Imagine Co-existence: Restoring Humanity after Violent Ethnic Conflict.* San Francisco: Jossey-Bass.

Coulter, S. (2001) Creating safety for trauma survivors: what can therapists do? *Journal of Child Care in Practice*, 7(1): 45–56.

Cronen, V. and Pearce, W.B. (1982) The co-ordinated management of meaning: a theory of communication, in F.E.X. Dance (ed.) *Human Communication Theory*. New York: Harper & Row.

Cronen, V., Johnson, K.M. and Lannamann, M.A. (1982) Paradoxes, double binds and reflexive loops: an alternative theoretical perspective, *Family Process*, 21(1): 91–112.

Fay, M.T., Morrissey, M. and Smyth, M. (1999) *Northern Ireland's Troubles: The Human Costs.* London: Pluto Press.

Healey, A. (2004) A different description of trauma: a wider systemic perspective – a personal insight, *Journal of Child Care in Practice*, 10(2): 167–84.

Herman, J.L. (1992) *Trauma and Recovery: From Domestic Abuse to Political Power.* London: Pandora.

Jarman, N. (2004) From war to peace? Changing patterns of violence in Northern Ireland, 1990–2003, in P. Shirlow and R. Monaghan (eds) *Terrorism and Political Violence – Special Issue: Northern Ireland Ten Years of Ceasefire*, 16(3): 420–38.

Kapur, R. (2001) Omagh: the beginning of the reparative impulse? *Psychoanalytic Psychotherapy*, 15(3): 265–78.

Landau, J. and Saul, J. (2004) Facilitating family and community resilience in response to major disaster, in F. Walsh and M. McGoldrick (eds) *Living Beyond Loss.* New York: Norton.

McCormick, M.M. (1997) Avoidance strategies in Northern Ireland, in D. Fry and K. Bjorkqvistj (eds) *Cultural Variation in Conflict Resolution*. Mahwah, NJ: Lawrence Erlbaum.

McKittrick, D., Kelters, S., Feeney, B. and Thornton, C. (1999) *Lost Lives: The Stories of Men, Women and Children who Died as a Result of the Northern Ireland Troubles*. London: Mainstream.

Office of the First Minister and Deputy First Minister (OFMDFM) (1998) *The Belfast Agreement: Agreement Reached in Multi-Party Negotiations*. Belfast: OFMDFM.

Office of the First Minister and Deputy First Minister (OFMDFM) (2005) *A Shared Future: Policy and Strategic Framework for Good Relations in Northern Ireland*. Belfast: OFMDFM.

Pearce, W.B. and Pearce, K.A. (1998) Transcendent storytelling: abilities for systemic practitioners and their clients, *Human Systems*, 9(3–4): (joint issue): 167–84.

Perlesz, A. (1999) Complex responses to trauma: challenges in bearing witness, *Australian and New Zealand Journal of Family Therapy*, 20(1): 11–19.

PSNI (2003) Persons injured as a result of the security situation in Northern Ireland 1969–2003 (by calendar year), in *Northern Ireland Annual Abstract of Statistics*. Belfast: The Stationery Office.

Reilly, I., McDermott, M. and Coulter, S. (2004) Living in the shadow of community violence in Northern Ireland: a therapeutic response, in N. Boyd Webb (ed.) *Mass Trauma and Violence: Helping Families and Children Cope*. New York: Guilford.

Sluzki, C. (2003) The process towards reconciliation, in A. Chayes and M. Minow (eds) *Imagine Co-existence: Restoring Humanity after Violent Ethnic Conflict*. San Francisco: Jossey-Bass.

Weingarten, K. (2000) Witnessing, wonder and hope, *Family Process*, 39(4): 389–402.

Weingarten, K. (2003) *Common Shock: How we are Hurt, How we can Heal*. New York: Dutton.

Part 3

Reflections on reconciliation and forgiveness

Chapter 10

The interactional process of forgiveness and responsibility: a critical assessment of the family therapy literature

Kerrie James

How important is it that we forgive those who have hurt us? Is forgiveness possible or even desirable in the absence of repentance on the part of the wrongdoer? By examining 'forgiveness' on the one hand and responsibility and atonement on the other, this chapter explores forgiveness as an interactional event rather than an intra-psychic process. It is argued that in the context of therapy, facilitating an injured party to forgive when a wrongdoer is neither repentant nor taking the necessary steps to atone for the injury, may pose significant risks to the injured party.

The literature portrays forgiveness as a process occurring primarily within an individual. McCullough identifies the elements common to various definitions proposed by forgiveness theorists: 'forgiveness is defined as intra-individual, pro-social change toward a perceived transgressor that is situated within a specific interpersonal context' (McCullough *et al.* 2000: 9). Forgiveness is often distinguished from 'pardoning', 'condoning', 'excusing', 'forgetting', 'denying' and 'reconciling'. Discourses of forgiveness and apology use the term 'injury' when referring to the action that is to be forgiven, and the term 'wrongdoer' when referring to the perpetrator of the injury. In this chapter, the terms 'injured party' or 'victim', and 'wrongdoer' or 'offender' are used.

Some writers argue that forgiveness can occur in the absence of reconciliation with the wrongdoer (Worthington and Drinkard 2000). Therefore, 'forgiveness' is viewed primarily as an 'intra-personal' process, i.e. occurring within the individual. While the experience of forgiving is psychological, it is also depicted as 'interpersonal' in that it involves forgiveness of another's wrongdoing (Exline and Baumeister 2000; McCullough *et al.* 2000). As forgiveness of oneself is also possible, the concept can also refer to forgiving an aspect of the self. In addition to these aspects, forgiveness can also be viewed as 'interactional'.

Couple and family therapy literature has encouraged therapists to use 'forgiveness' as a way to resolve bitterness resulting from interpersonal 'injuries' and 'wounds' (Gordon *et al.* 2000; Hill 2001; Butler *et al.* 2002; Murray 2002; Olson *et al.* 2002; Tomm 2002). In fact, bitterness and the lack of forgiveness is sometimes viewed as the underlying problem, which becomes the focus of therapy. In these cases 'the focus is to resolve the heart of the problem by encouraging a healthy letting go of vengeance and records of wrong' (DiBlasio and Proctor 1993: 176).

Many discussions of forgiveness imply that the ability or willingness of an individual to 'let go' and forgive is a salient personality characteristic of the individual, viewed as a virtue or ability and juxtaposed against 'bitterness' or 'holding a grudge' (DiBlasio and Proctor 1993). It is claimed that forgiveness augurs well for an individual's health and well-being. Compared to holding grudges, or carrying unresolved anger towards others, the act of forgiving and the letting go of resentments is seen as a more enlightened and desirable way of being (Davis 2002; Spring 2004). Forgiveness is the goal of therapeutic intervention, whereas wrongdoer responsibility, apology and atonement or, in the words of Worthington, 'confess, apologize and repent' are viewed as desirable, but inessential, steps along the way (Worthington and Drinkard 2000: 97). Forgiveness on the part of the injured person, not responsibility on the part of the wrongdoer, is the usual aim of therapy. It is tempting to postulate some reasons for this. Victims are perhaps easier to work with, being more likely to request help and elicit empathy from therapists. Wrongdoers, on the other hand, are less likely to seek help of their own volition and are more likely to act defensively when they do (Tomm 2002). Whatever the reason, the apparent skewing of psychological literature towards the injured party's forgiveness at best eclipses the importance of therapists attending to wrongdoer responsibility and, at worst, encourages therapists to expect victims to forgive in the absence of wrongdoer accountability.

Gordon *et al.* (2000: 213), in their review of the literature on forgiveness, argue that most models of forgiveness have the following goals:

- to help the injured party regain a more balanced view of the offender and the event;
- to assist them to decrease negative affect toward the offender;
- to encourage them to give up the right to punish the offender further.

There appear to be three major interventions to facilitate these goals: structured forgiveness interventions, couple therapy approaches and family therapy models that integrate forgiveness and/or apology sessions within ongoing family sessions. Family therapy approaches can be further divided into two camps: those that emphasize apology or those that emphasize forgiveness. The degree to which wrongdoer responsibility is addressed as a component of the forgiveness process in each of these approaches is explored in the following sections.

Structured forgiveness interventions for groups or individuals

Most models of forgiveness involve structured psycho-educational methods for use with groups (often couples) or with individuals. Their aim is to facilitate forgiveness independently of whether or not the wrongdoer has admitted responsibility, apologized or atoned (Enright and the Human Development Study Group 1991; Freedman 2000; Worthington *et al.* 2000; Freedman and Knupp 2003). People who want to forgive, and who want to be relieved of resentment, anger and sometimes guilt may be assisted by these approaches to reach an internal state of forgiveness, regardless of whether the wrongdoer has atoned, and independently of whether the relationship is continuing. What is not addressed in this literature is the issue of what happens to people who are unable to forgive despite taking these steps. One wonders to what extent they turn against themselves, adding layers to the self-blame they already feel in relation to the original injury.

Couples therapy interventions

Couples who bear grudges for unresolved injuries they inflict on each other are viewed as ripe for a focus on forgiveness. A number of studies have elaborated on the forgiveness process in relation to extramarital affairs. An approach called 'decision-based forgiveness treatment' is often used in cases of marital infidelity (Worthington and DiBlasio 1990; Gordon and Baucom 1998; Gordon *et al.* 2000; Olson *et al.* 2002). Others have focused on apology and forgiveness as a component of reconciliation in situations of interpersonal injury or insult, devaluation of partner, lack of respect, failure to agree on an important topic, emotional distancing and cut-off (Worthington and Drinkard 2000).

With the goal of forgiveness, therapy emphasizes the injured party's role in healing the rift in the relationship. Less often the emphasis is on the wrongdoer, or the wrongdoer's role in healing the rift. Likewise, couple researchers concentrate on forgiveness, not on wrongdoer responsibility, apology or atonement (Enright and the Human Development Study Group 1991; Hargrave and Sells 1997; Gordon *et al.* 2000). It is not that apology and responsibility of the wrongdoer is ignored, but the actions of the wrongdoer are viewed as being in the service of achieving forgiveness from the injured party, and it is forgiveness that is viewed as the quintessential element in healing relationships.

Gordon and Baucom (1998) have developed a model of forgiveness therapy to help couples heal their relationships after betrayal. While the authors acknowledge that the wrongdoer has a significant role in the forgiveness process (having to convey a clear signal of remorse in order for trust to be restored), its main emphasis is on the value of forgiving for the injured party.

Curiously, the person who committed the betrayal is termed the 'participating partner' rather than the wrongdoer. Perhaps this is done to minimize the negative connotations of 'wrongdoer' when applied to someone whose actions may be in response to an unhappy marriage or partnership. Perhaps the negative connotation of 'wrongdoer', particularly in situations of affairs, does carry too heavy a burden. However, the use of 'participating partner' may err too far in the opposite direction. The idea of 'participation' implies that the offender merely contributed to an action that these same authors later describe as constituting a 'trauma' for the injured party. Baucom and Gordon do assert, however, that 'it is the participating partner who is responsible for making the decision to engage in that act', which would seem to imply something more than just 'participation' (Gordon *et al.* 2000: 435).

Family therapy approaches

In the family therapy literature there has been increasing interest in the area of forgiveness and apology. This interest has coalesced around healing relationships within adults' families of origin, including issues such as partner affairs, domestic violence, child abuse and the myriad of attachment injuries occurring within couple and family relationships. Family therapists bring family members face to face to focus on either forgiveness or apology (Trepper and Barrett 1989; Madanes 1990; Hargrave 1994; DiBlasio 1998; MacKinnon 1998; Walrond-Skinner 1998; Worthington 1998; Hill 2001; Sheinberg and Fraenkel 2001).

DiBlasio (1998) has developed a 'forgiveness intervention' for use in family therapy. This is a planned session, where family members admit whatever wrongdoings they have committed, seek and give forgiveness to others. The therapist meets with each family member in turn, helping each to identify the wrongdoings for which they are seeking forgiveness. Then the family session is held, and each person asks for forgiveness.

It is implied in this approach that 'owning up' to wrongdoings is the same as taking responsibility and that this opens the way to focus on forgiveness. The nature and impact of the wrongdoings do not appear to be dwelt upon, nor whether the degree to which each person's remorse is either genuine or based on empathy for the victim. In situations of abuse or severe injury, this type of approach would favour an offender who was keen to 'apologize' in order to resume the relationship, and who wished to avoid more in-depth examination of his or her wrongdoing. It could also result in a victim experiencing pressure to forgive a repentant wrongdoer (Walrond-Skinner 1998). Similar concerns can be raised about Worthington's approach described in his 'empathy–humility–commitment model' of forgiveness, where the focus is on 'how to induce clients to grant forgiveness by therapeutic and psycho-educational interventions' and where 'forgiveness is initiated by empathy for the offender, furthered by humility in the person who was hurt and solidified through making a public commitment to forgiveness' (Worthington 1998: 63). Such an approach might be appropriate if certain conditions are met such as the injured person's desire to keep the relationship with the wrongdoer, the offences being assessed as falling on the less serious end of the continuum and where there are minimal power differences between wrongdoer and victim.

Contextual family therapy emphasizes forgiveness as a significant component of healing intergenerational wounds and resolving violations of trust (Sandberg 1999). Hargrave (1994) views both forgiveness and apology as the 'warp' and 'weft' of the session, the therapist eliciting one then the other as the exploration of each person's experience unfolds. Hargrave facilitates forgiveness by encouraging the wrongdoer to validate the injured party's experience, acknowledge the wrongdoing and its impact and undertake restitution. Hargrave also emphasizes the responsibility of the 'wrongdoer' to make amends by acknowledging responsibility, making compensation and apologizing (Hargrave 1994; Hargrave and Sells 1997). Here the onus is placed upon the injured party to notice and acknowledge efforts on the part of the wrongdoer to make restitution. This is viewed as a 'gift' to the wrongdoer, and indicates that the injured party is willing to let go of vengeance or revenge. What is not explored is the effect of this type of approach on the victim. One assumes that the injured party is not feeling pressured into giving the wrongdoer another chance, and is genuinely seeking to use the therapy to heal the relationship with the wrongdoer.

In contrast to the extensive attention forgiveness has attracted in the family therapy field, there has been very little written on the subject of repentance, responsibility for wrongdoing, apology or atonement with the notable exception of Hargrave who, as noted above, does facilitate the wrongdoer's apology. In general, literature addressing domestic violence and child abuse is more likely to focus upon wrongdoer accountability and responsibility. In fact, all of the approaches that advocate responsibility and apology over forgiveness have been developed in relation to child sexual assault or domestic violence (Madanes 1990; MacKinnon 1998; Sheinberg and Fraenkel 2001). These models explicitly advocate apology, while forgiveness is either not advocated or just not addressed.

In situations of child sexual assault, a victim's healing hinges on the offender (and sometimes the non-offending parent) taking full responsibility for the abuse, relieving the child from the burden of guilt and responsibility they otherwise often assume (Verco 2002). If a victim wishes to work towards healing their relationship with the offender, offender responsibility, atonement and apology come into focus. Madanes (1990) for instance is very clear that the victim of sexual assault should not be expected to forgive the perpetrator. In dealing with both adult and juvenile sex offenders, Madanes requires the offender to get on their knees and apologize for the offence: 'When the offender gets on his knees and expresses sorrow for what he has done, the victim can forgive him if she wants to but she does not have to forgive. There should be no pressure on the victim' (1990: 54). The offender is also expected to undertake some kind of reparation to underscore his repentance and to facilitate the victim's healing.

Trepper and Barrett (1989), in their classic text on systemic treatment of incest, describe the apology session, where the father apologizes to the child, taking full responsibility for the abuse he has perpetrated. There is no expectation that the child will forgive the father, in fact the term 'forgiveness' and its synonyms do not appear in the index. This is also the case with the approaches advocated by MacKinnon (1998) and Sheinberg and Fraenkel (2001). Similar emphasis on the wrongdoer's accountability for acts of violence and abuse is evident within most approaches to working with domestic violence (Almeida and Bograd 1990; Goldner *et al.* 1990).

Problems with the emphasis on forgiveness

It is curious that despite research that indicates that people are much more likely to forgive if the wrongdoer has taken responsibility, offered sincere apology and atoned for the offence, therapeutic literature emphasizes facilitating forgiveness rather than 'owning up' and apologizing (Exline and Baumeister 2000). Models of forgiveness argue that forgiveness is a good thing, a worthwhile goal of intervention. Rarely is a voice raised in dissent. The exception, as we have seen, is the literature in family therapy on abuse and trauma, where emphasis is on protecting the victim from the offender, on not expecting the victim to forgive and on emphasizing the offender's accountability. In fact, it is interesting to speculate that authors who focus on child abuse or domestic violence are more likely to emphasize the responsibility of the wrongdoer in healing an ongoing relationship, whereas those who focus more on couple betrayals seem to focus more on forgiveness.

Within mainstream family therapy, there has also been resistance to using forgiveness interventions. Sue Walrond-Skinner (1998) cites three concerns held by family therapists: firstly, that the traditional location of forgiveness is within the discourse of religious and theological thought; secondly, the concern that a focus on forgiveness would 'compound the problem of the disappearing victim' (p. 6) through unwarranted exoneration of the perpetrator in the case of abuse; and thirdly, the concern that forgiveness could be used defensively to protect a wrongdoer or used by the victim to deny their own anger. The following section explores these and other concerns about a focus on forgiveness as a goal in family therapy.

Promoting forgiveness without regard to the severity of the injury

The literature promoting forgiveness makes no distinctions as to what should or should not be forgiven, or what could or could not be forgiven. This is often because forgiveness is viewed as an individual experience and is often discussed without reference to the nature of the specific offence or injury.

Therapists play a significant role in naming actual wrongdoings and assessing the severity of injuries. There is general agreement among therapists that the perpetration of domestic violence and sexual assault is more likely to result in injuries that are severe to the point of causing lasting trauma. While other injuries are not so easily classified as to seriousness, the victim's experience of wrongdoing should be assessed in terms of the degree of shock, betrayal and trauma incurred. Sometimes factors other than the injury itself mediate how a victim experiences the severity of an injury, such as victim resilience, the experience of previous injuries, cognitive beliefs about the offence, degree of intentionality or the significance of the offender to the victim. These victim variables, however, should not be used to hasten a victim's forgiveness or exoneration of an injury, but should be used to help the wrongdoer understand the even greater need for vigilance in not re-offending or re-injuring the victim. Therapists need to identify and acknowledge specific injuries and their severity in order to validate the client's experience and contextualize the client's reaction to the injury.

Promoting forgiveness without regard to the likelihood of the offence recurring

Forgiving a wrongdoer for a transgression may have either no deterrent effect on a wrongdoer's re-offending, or may even encourage the likelihood of further transgressions. Exline and Baumeister (2000:144) point out that repeated transgressions are especially likely in interpersonal environments characterized by hostility and mistrust and that victims could legitimately fear being hurt again by people who are distant or not highly motivated to protect the victim's well-being. Therefore, encouraging someone to forgive a wrong, without an assessment of the relationship, may be inviting further injury. Victims who want to reconcile with an offender may forgive prematurely in order to keep a valued relationship. Their motivation is based on fear of loss, rather than an assessment of the likely impact of forgiveness on possible recurrence of the offence.

In some situations, it may not be wise for a victim to grant forgiveness to a wrongdoer. A victim's withholding of forgiveness actually gives her or him leverage. Not forgiving can underscore the seriousness of the offence and give time to an offender to consider the impact of the transgression and how they might make amends. In this sense, forgiveness is earned by the wrongdoer and is not freely given.

Some have addressed the above concerns by distinguishing 'forgiveness' from both 'pardoning' and 'reconciliation'. Butler argues that forgiveness can have a number of motivations, and that forgiveness in the interests of personal or spiritual growth can be granted or encouraged, without either pardoning the wrongdoer or reconciling the relationship (Butler *et al.* 2002: 285). It is possible, however, that any focus on forgiveness, even for personal or spiritual growth, may translate as pardoning the offender or as condoning the wrongdoing, regardless of attempts to distinguish between these motivations.

An example is the frequency with which many women prematurely forgive partners in situations of domestic violence. Domestic violence is a wrongdoing that is more likely to be forgiven, whereas sexual violence is less likely to be forgiven (Butler *et al.* 2002: 294). In domestic violence situations, forgiveness may function to exonerate the wrongdoer. In couples counselling, therapist and victim may both collude to deny, and thus protect, the wrongdoer from experiencing shame. An abused woman may forgive her abuser out of fear of losing the relationship if she were to hold him accountable. When a victim's reaction is understated in relation to a first offence it is more likely that a wrongdoer will repeat his violence, even more severely. In contrast, if a victim's reaction is strong and firm, that is, she immediately leaves the relationship, names the abuse and involves the police, it is less likely (though not impossible) that he will abuse her again.

Therefore, a victim's forgiveness of a wrongdoing that is not earned by the wrongdoer poses a degree of risk to the victim. Prior to supporting a victim to forgive, an assessment of the victim's motivations as well as the likely consequences of forgiveness needs to be undertaken.

Promoting forgiveness without regard to safety

It follows from the above concerns that victims who grant forgiveness to wrongdoers who have not earned it may be putting themselves at risk of further injury. Therefore, risk needs to be assessed in relation to whether a victim forgives a wrongdoer with whom they are in a continuing relationship, or whether forgiveness itself leads to a relationship continuing.

'Reconciliation' usually refers to both parties resuming their relationship. It is often argued that 'forgiveness' does not have to lead to or imply 'reconciliation'. However, although not necessarily related, reconciliation often gives a message of forgiveness to the wrongdoer, whether or not the victim intends this. Worthington and Drinkard (2000: 93) specify that the 'the restoration of trust in an interpersonal relationship through mutual trustworthy behaviours' is the essential component of reconciliation. One might question why they would use the term 'mutual' given that there is usually a wrongdoer and a victim, and it is the wrongdoer who needs to be demonstrating trustworthiness. Actually, it is often in situations where abuse has occurred that people reconcile in the absence of these trustworthy behaviours.

Equalizing injuries regardless of severity or power differentials between victim and offender

Sometimes forgiveness is held as a general goal for both wrongdoer and victim, as if the playing field can be equalized through sharing the wrong-doings. When forgiveness is promoted as an intervention in this way, it is assumed that everyone within the family has been injured and has something to forgive, or that each person is both victim and perpetrator. While in part this recognizes that wrongdoers also have injuries that need to be addressed, the collapsing of these roles in relation to serious transgressions may be unfair to the injured party and pander to perpetrators justifying their actions in terms of 'provocation' by victims. With the exception of extra-marital affairs, there is often little reference to the nature of the relationship within which the injury occurred and therefore the meaning of the injury to the victim. Therapists need to maintain clarity about who is the victim and who is the transgressor in relation to each injury, as well as bearing in mind the relative differences in severity of injuries.

When wrongdoers see themselves as victims, a focus on forgiveness can inadvertently reinforce the defensive denial of harmful behaviour. Minimally, having a frame of responsibility rather than forgiveness helps each party examine and take responsibility for their own actions and their consequences without equating the severity of injuries. The therapist's goal is to draw out the power differential, for instance different amounts of fear, different options for escape. The aim in situations of mutual allegations is for the more serious transgressor to take responsibility, atone and apologize first, so that there is less risk of serious offences being minimized. The therapist needs to be clear about the relative severity of injuries, the relationship context in which they occurred and the need for safety to be restored before a victim's own transgressions are addressed.

Pressure to forgive

Walrond-Skinner has argued that 'forgiveness may be inappropriately urged upon victims with the effect (intended or not) of releasing the perpetrator from responsibility for his actions' (1998: 9). There are dangers for victims as a result of experiencing pressure to forgive, regardless of whether the pressure comes from the offender, family members, therapists or others (Tomm 2002: 67). They may feel as if they have to deny their own anger and sense of injustice. If they resist forgiving, they risk being viewed negatively by others and may lose valued relationships as people side with the wrongdoer. Furthermore, they may view themselves negatively because they are either unable or unwilling to forgive.

Caution needs to be exercised where a victim's lack of forgiveness involves a desire for control, revenge or retaliation, especially if the victim occupies a position of power in relation to the wrongdoer, or has a distorted view of themselves as victims. For example, a violent man in a rage about his partner's affair might indeed be a victim in relation to this wrongdoing. However, she is also a victim in relation to his violence and is at more significant risk. Equating these injuries or encouraging the man to withhold forgiveness until his wife recanted would constitute a serious mistake. The goal should be a focus on the more serious injury of intimidation and violence.

Conclusion

The therapeutic literature is biased towards promoting forgiveness and does not fully take account of the nature or severity of injuries, relationships between victims and wrongdoers, or the impact on wrongdoers of forgiveness. The relationship between apology and forgiveness is rarely viewed interactionally and victims are often expected to forgive in the absence of wrongdoer accountability.

Family therapists are in a unique position to help families heal relationships that have been harmed by abuse, violence, interpersonal betrayals and a host of other acts that result in relationship breakdown. Despite the challenge posed to therapists when both parties claim to be victims, it is the responsibility of therapists to assess each person's claims and hold wrongdoers accountable. Forgiveness as a primary goal should only be pursued in situations where there is no possibility of the wrongdoer taking responsibility, and as a goal it should not be 'recommended' to clients who are struggling with serious abuse injuries. If a person does move towards forgiveness as a result of therapy, the impact on the wrongdoer needs to be assessed in terms of any likely repetition or minimization of the injury, remembering that experiencing forgiveness and actually conveying forgiveness are not the same.

One of the most potent and effective ways of healing hurt feelings in relationships is through wrongdoers taking responsibility, apologizing and making atonement. The wrongdoer's actions are pivotal in enabling an injured party to forgive, and for the possible restoration of the relationship. In this sense, the *sine qua non* of healing is responsibility, atonement and apology, not forgiveness.

References

Almeida, R. and Bograd, M. (1990) Sponsorship, holding men accountable for domestic violence, *Journal of Feminist Family Therapy*, 2(3–4): 234–56.

Butler, M., Dahlin, S. and Fife, S. (2002) 'Languaging' factors affecting clients' acceptance of forgiveness intervention in marital therapy, *Journal of Marital and Family Therapy*, 28(3): 285–98.

Davis, L. (2002) *I Thought We'd Never Speak Again: Strategies for Healing Broken Relationships*. London: Vermilion.

DiBlasio, F. (1998) The use of decision-based forgiveness intervention within intergenerational family therapy, *Journal of Family Therapy*, 20(1): 77–94.

DiBlasio, F. and Proctor, J. (1993) Therapists and the clinical use of forgiveness, *The American Journal of Family Therapy*, 21(2): 175–84.

Enright, R.D. and the Human Development Study Group (1991) The moral development of forgiveness, in W. Kurtines and J. Gewirtz (eds) *Handbook of Moral Behavior and Development Volume 1*. Mahwah, NJ: Erlbaum.

Exline, J. and Baumeister, R. (2000) Expressing forgiveness and repentance: benefits and barriers, in M.E. McCullough, K.I. Pargament and C.E. Thoresen (eds) *Forgiveness: Theory, Research and Practice*. New York: Guilford.

Freedman, S. (2000) Creating an expanded view: how therapists can help their clients forgive, *Journal of Family Psychotherapy*, 11(1): 87–92.

Freedman, S. and Knupp, A. (2003) The impact of forgiveness on adolescent adjustment to parental divorce, *Journal of Divorce and Remarriage*, 39(1/2): 135–65.

Goldner, V., Penn, P., Sheinberg, M. and Walker, G. (1990) Love and violence: gender paradoxes in violent attachments, *Family Process*, 29(4): 343–64.

Gordon, K. and Baucom, D. (1998) Understanding betrayals in marriage: a synthesized model of forgiveness, *Family Process*, 37(4): 425–540.

Gordon, K., Baucom, D. and Snyder, K. (2000) The use of forgiveness in marital therapy, in M.E. McCullough, K.I. Pargament and C.E. Thoresen (eds) *Forgiveness: Theory, Research and Practice*. New York: Guilford.

Hargrave, T. (1994) *Families and Forgiveness*. New York: Brunner-Mazel.

Hargrave, T. and Sells, J. (1997) The development of a forgiveness scale, *Journal of Marital and Family Therapy*, 23(1): 41–6.

Hill, W. (2001) Understanding forgiveness as discovery: implications for marital and family therapy, *Contemporary Family Therapy: An International Journal*, 23(4): 369–84.

McCullough, M.E., Pargament, K.I. and Thoresen, C.E. (2000) *Forgiveness: Theory, Research and Practice*. New York: Guilford.

MacKinnon, L. (1998) *Trust and Betrayal in the Treatment of Child Abuse*. New York: Guilford.

Madanes, C. (1990) *Sex, Love and Violence*. New York: W.W. Norton.

Murray, R. (2002) Forgiveness as a therapeutic option, *Family Journal: Counseling and Therapy for Couples and Families*, 10(3): 315–21.

Olson, M., Russell, C., Higgins-Kessler, M. and Miller, R. (2002) Emotional processes following disclosure of an extramarital affair, *Journal of Marital and Family Therapy*, 28(4): 423–34.

Sandberg, J. (1999) 'It just isn't fair': helping older families balance their ledgers before the note comes due, *Family Relations*, 48(2): 177–9.

Sheinberg, M. and Fraenkel, P. (2001) *The Relational Trauma of Incest*. New York: Guilford.

Spring, J. (2004) *How Can I Forgive You?* New York: HarperCollins.

Tomm, K. (2002) Enabling forgiveness and reconciliation in family therapy, *The International Journal of Narrative Therapy and Community Work*, 1: 65–9.

Trepper, T. and Barrett, M. (1989) *Systemic Treatment of Incest*. New York: Brunner-Mazel.

Verco, J. (2002) Women's outrage and the pressure to forgive, *The International Journal of Narrative Therapy and Community Work*, 1: 23–7.

Walrond-Skinner, S. (1998) The function and role of forgiveness in working with couples and families, *Journal of Family Therapy*, 20(1): 3–20.

Worthington, E. (1998) An empathy-humility-commitment model of forgiveness applied within family dyads, *Journal of Family Therapy*, 20(1): 59–76.

Worthington, E. and DiBlasio, F. (1990) Promoting mutual forgiveness within the fractured relationship, *Psychotherapy*, 27(2): 219–23.

Worthington, E. and Drinkard, D. (2000) Promoting reconciliation through psycho-educational and therapeutic interventions, *Journal of Marital and Family Therapy*, 26(1): 93–102.

Worthington, E., Sandage, S. and Berry, J. (2000) Group interventions to promote forgiveness, in M.E. McCullough, K.I. Pargament and C.E. Thoresen (eds) *Forgiveness: Theory, Research and Practice*. New York: Guilford.

Chapter 11

Acknowledgement: its significance for reconciliation and well-being

Karl Tomm and Trudy Govier

When people live in mutually supportive relationships they have a solid basis for ongoing hopefulness. However, when relationships deteriorate through disappointments, betrayals or traumatic events, interpersonal stress and conflict tend to displace the support. As a result, hope may be eroded and the persons involved become more vulnerable to despair. Possibilities for rebuilding and maintaining hope increase when people develop behavioural competencies to recover from conflict and achieve reconciliation. We suggest that practices of acknowledgement constitute one such competency. Indeed, we regard processes of acknowledging as central, not only for enabling reconciliation (Tomm 2002), but also for generating and maintaining human wellness. The focus in this chapter will be on the phenomenon of acknowledgement itself. Our intent is to offer some clarifying distinctions to enhance the reader's interest, understanding and competence in offering acknowledgement.

What is acknowledgement?

As the term suggests, acknowledgement is knowledge plus something else. The something else is the respectful expression of that knowledge to someone. The expression conveys a move toward greater respect for the recipient. The prefix 'ac' in the word 'acknowledgement' is an adaptation of the Latin word *ad*, which means 'to', 'towards' or 'added to'. Acknowledgement is an explicit expression of something already known (by the speaker at least) which is communicated to another person, and sometimes to a whole community. It usually occurs as a process of articulation through which some particular knowledge is brought into clear awareness, to stand out in sharp relief, to be attended to and responded to. Some acknowledgements are conveyed through non-verbal gestures (thumbs up, a wave of the hand) or through attendance at social rituals to honour a person or group (graduations, weddings, opening ceremonies). But most are expressed in words.

Acts of acknowledgment are common, and as such can easily be overlooked and taken for granted. For instance, whenever we greet another person, we acknowledge them. When we applaud something or someone, we implicitly acknowledge the event or performance as noteworthy. Partners in committed relationships often acknowledge their love for one another, to explicitly reaffirm their mutual commitment. Attentive parents and teachers regularly acknowledge the achievements of children to support their development. We also acknowledge whenever we admit having made mistakes. In other words, acknowledgements abound among us as human beings.

Acknowledgement is essentially a relational phenomenon: people acknowledge when they express their knowledge *to* someone. There is always that 'to' element, even when the acknowledgement is to oneself, as distinct from another person. Thus, there must always be a receiver when something is acknowledged. The receiver, typically a listener, is attentive to the speaker and actively gives meaning to what is being spoken. The listener recognizes that the knowledge expressed has significance for their relationship with the person acknowledging. They usually convey receptiveness, often by acknowledging the acknowledgement, so they jointly co-construct mutual respect. Thus acknowledgement can be said to be an inter-subjective phenomenon: both speaker and listener participate actively in the process. If a person were passively observing an acknowledgement, not responding to it in any way, then the generative aspect of respectful meaning-making, so basic to acknowledging, would not arise.

The person acknowledging actively gives a particular meaning to their knowledge in the process of expressing it and the person receiving the acknowledgement gives serious consideration to the meaning being conveyed. For the recipient, an acknowledgement either brings something new into existence, or makes something already known become more immediate and 'real'. If the recipient's prior knowledge was subconscious or incomplete, that knowledge becomes more conscious or full. If the knowledge was already fully present in the recipient, explicit acknowledgement still serves the purpose of validating that knowledge to become more consensual and firmly established. Overall, the vividness of a specified reality is enhanced and the degree to which the same knowledge is held in common by both speaker and listener is increased.

This process of bringing something more fully into existence and consensual awareness is a fundamental aspect of acknowledgement, an aspect that contributes to the construction and maintenance of the social realities in which we live. It is an example of social construction in action. While every act of communication could be broadly construed as an act of acknowledgement, broadening the concept of acknowledgement in this way is unhelpful because it obscures the social constructionist effects of acknowledging and distracts us from the significance of conveying respect towards the other, in the action we take with our knowledge.

Interestingly, the verb 'to acknowledge' is a performative one. In normal contexts (outside the realm of acting and storytelling) if I *say* 'I acknowledge ...', I do, by saying so, thereby acknowledge. It is more proactive to say 'I acknowledge I made a mistake' than to say 'I made a mistake' – even though the latter still counts as an acknowledgement. As a performative, the verb 'to acknowledge' resembles the verb 'to promise'. It is dissimilar to other verbs such as 'to forgive'. Forgiving is not performative: a person can say that they forgive without actually doing so. One who says 'I forgive you' but goes on being resentful has not in fact forgiven, despite their words (Govier 2002). The word 'acknowledge' need not be used to acknowledge something, but if it is, the acknowledgement tends to be stronger, due to the performative effect.

Three types of acknowledgement

An act of acknowledgement can focus primarily on recognizing the existence of a person as a whole or a particular action or characteristic of that person. The former focus may be referred to as 'existential acknowledgement'. In this form of acknowledgement, one is articulating one's recognition that the person exists and merits consideration. A specific action or characteristic of a person, on the other hand, may be regarded as either positive or negative. When it is valued positively, acknowledgement of it may be described as 'affirming acknowledgement'. When it is valued negatively, acknowledgement of it may be described as 'aversive acknowledgement'. Positive or affirming acknowledgement may include drawing attention to a contribution, achievement, privilege, talent, admirable personality trait or other feature regarded as positive. Negative or aversive acknowledgement may include drawing attention to a crisis, failure, mistake, wrongdoing, personal flaw, unwanted habit or other feature regarded as negative. Affirming and aversive acknowledgements do, of course, have some existential implications. To possess a feature – positive or negative – a person must already exist. (One cannot draw attention to a characteristic without presupposing, and thereby committing oneself to, the existence of the person.) However, existential acknowledgement can still be said to differ from both affirming and aversive acknowledgement, given that existential acknowledgement focuses more directly on the legitimacy of a person. All three types of acknowledgement may be extended towards groups, nations, organizations, events, objects and processes.

Existential acknowledgement can be relatively neutral when it pertains to objects or events, but tends to be affirming when it pertains to a person. A man who acknowledges a woman implicitly conveys legitimacy to her existence in relation to himself. To have one's person, being, or identity acknowledged in some way is to feel that one exists more fully, that one has more substance and in a sense more 'reality' has been added to one's life. Given that people do exist and regard themselves as legitimate entities in the world, existential acknowledgement has positive effects. For that reason, it can be said to overlap with affirming acknowledgement. People do not like to be treated as though they do not exist; a corollary is that they appreciate having their existence acknowledged. Persons so acknowledged often experience themselves as enlivened and energized, in part because they have been recognized and legitimized.

Like other forms of acknowledgement, existential acknowledgement can be offered to groups, communities, organizations, nations, races, etc. Gays and lesbians are increasingly being acknowledged as legitimate not only as individuals but also as groups. Indeed, we will be so bold as to assert that acknowledgement of the existence of another person or group is *never* unimportant.

Affirming acknowledgement, when person-centred, contributes directly and deliberately to the recipient's psychological and emotional well-being. The ubiquitous 'thank you' is an example. Commenting on something one admires or appreciates about another person is another. When something about oneself is recognized, genuinely valued and explicitly acknowledged, one simply feels good. Indeed, most interpersonal relationships, whether personal or professional, are more gratifying and enjoyable when affirming acknowledgement is regularly part of the interaction. Couple researchers have shown that marital satisfaction and marriage survival are correlated with the frequency of affirming and validating statements that spouses make to one another on a daily basis.

Affirming acknowledgement can come from a variety of sources, including from oneself. To acknowledge one's own constructive qualities, initiatives and contributions *to oneself* is a means of maintaining one's self-esteem. The movement toward appreciative enquiry entails a process of drawing out and acknowledging personally affirming experiences, and has been used in many communities to enable transformations from negative attitudes and practices to more positive ones. Affirming acknowledgement is, of course, a major theme that runs through the gamut of resource-oriented psychotherapies. Therapists and reflecting teams working from this perspective give priority not only to affirming constructive qualities and initiatives in their clients, but also to affirming the clients' patterns of affirming themselves and others. The practices of reinforcing preferred behaviours and selectively 'naming with approval' are often taught to parents to strengthen their ability to nurture their children's self-esteem and personal development.

At first glance, *aversive acknowledgement* might seem to be more harmful than helpful; it draws attention to something that is negative. No one is likely to enjoy having to face problems, inadequacies or allegations of wrongdoing. Criticism and blame may be regarded as harmful and counterproductive forms of aversive acknowledgement. And yet, aversive acknowledgement that is authentic and respectful can be extremely valuable as a step towards reconciliation (Tomm 2002) and personal and social well-being. Some criticisms deserve attention and taking them seriously (Govier 2002) can result in constructive changes. It is only when people recognize and acknowledge a problem that deliberate action can be taken in relation to it. At an individual level, a person who denies that they have a serious problem like diabetes, alcoholism, depression or aggressiveness cannot begin to address that problem. Because the disorder is unpleasant and unwelcome, they would no doubt prefer to ignore it but they will do so at their own peril. Aversive acknowledgement is also important in collective contexts. Social injustices like racism, slavery, sexism, heterosexism, poverty and ethnocentrism need to be recognized and openly acknowledged as problems; if they are not, plans for affirmative action cannot be developed or implemented.

With regard to interpersonal conflict, acknowledgement of an act of wrongdoing is usually a crucial first step toward reconciliation. If one person has wronged another and is not willing to acknowledge that, the person harmed will be fearful that the wrongs could be committed again, and will be unable to trust and work towards an improved relationship. Apology is a familiar form of aversive acknowledgement that generally creates favourable conditions for reconciliation. Extending a genuine apology to someone is to acknowledge that one has done wrong. If a father apologizes to his daughter for abusing her as a child, he acknowledges that he committed the act, that he did wrong and that he is accepting responsibility for having done so. In allowing that what he did was wrong, he is, in effect, recognizing that she did not deserve to be abused, and that she deserved better. Thus, his aversive acknowledgement implies an affirming acknowledgement of her worth and confers respect.

For a victim who receives such acknowledgement some important aspects of healing can begin to occur. Their experience of abuse is validated and they are relieved of the anxiety of wondering whether they could be imagining that these things were done. They will be spared the burden of attempting to convince others that their experience of having been abused was not the product of their imagination. The disturbing experience, which was previously unrecognized by many, has now been *acknowledged* in the apology. In a sense, the pain and suffering have been made more real; they can be said to be legitimized in the sense that we would expect anyone who had been treated in this way to experience harm and to suffer. Given the acknowledgement, the abuse has been given an outward, public dimension. The effect of this public aspect is that the inner reality of the victim becomes more coherent with an outer public world. Consequently, they become more grounded in a consensual reality about what happened and that it was inappropriate.

While apology is an important form of aversive acknowledgement, it is not the only way in which such acknowledgement can be expressed. A husband can acknowledge that he made some bad choices in paying attention to another woman but still not apologize to his wife. In some political situations, such as those of the Acadians and the Japanese-Canadians, groups have been offered statements of acknowledgement that have not at the same time been apologies – thus highlighting the fact that apology is not, strictly speaking, necessary for aversive acknowledgement. Although moral apology offers acknowledgement, the converse is not true. Not every aversive acknowledgement comes in the form of an apology, although a formal apology has stronger effects than an acknowledgement unaccompanied by an apology.

A person who has been wronged, and is suffering from it, is likely to experience a powerful sense of *vindication* when a wrongdoer offers acknowledgement. On the other hand, an unacknowledged offence carries the implication that the victim deserved no better (Govier 2002) and therefore has little worth; i.e. a personal insult accompanies the injury. The insult is the message that it is perfectly all right to treat the person in this way: they are worthy of nothing better. Acknowledgement takes back that insult, saying in effect that 'you did not deserve this. You deserved better. I was wrong to do it'. It is an enormous relief to have an insult withdrawn through an acknowledgement and to have a sense of reality consensually restored – to have an admission that this hurtful thing really did happen, that it really was wrong, and that it really should not have happened. It is in this sense that aversive acknowledgement offers vindication and respect to the victim: 'you thought you were wronged, you thought you deserved to be treated with more respect; and in these beliefs, you were correct'. Acknowledgement that wrongs were committed also implies an intention and/or commitment not to do those things again. For those who have suffered the consequences of wrongdoing, acknowledgement that certain actions were done and should not have been done offers reassurance and a basis for rebuilding some *trust*.

Intrapersonal acknowledgement

Typically, acknowledgement occurs as a verbal transaction between two or more people and is interpersonal. However, in many circumstances it may occur upon reflection and take place within an individual person so that it is intrapersonal. As indicated earlier, something can be acknowledged *to* the self. Indeed, all three types of acknowledgement may be used to make positive changes in oneself.

Existential acknowledgement to oneself is a way to stabilize and maintain changes in one's identity during the life cycle. Changes in identity usually begin as acknowledgements in a community and then are maintained intrapersonally. For instance, in a marriage ceremony one's identity changes from being single to being married. Concurrently, expectations change about one's relationships with others. The husband may subsequently acknowledge to himself repeatedly that he is now committed to his wife and is no longer single, as a way to help maintain appropriate social and sexual boundaries.

Aversive acknowledgement to oneself that something is wrong or one has made a mistake is the first step to open possibilities for new learning and corrective initiatives. For instance, if a husband recognizes an imbalance of workload in household chores as a factor in his wife's unhappiness and acknowledges his 'laziness' to himself he is more liable to consider doing more.

Affirming acknowledgement to oneself is a helpful way to keep on course after having made a choice to change. For instance, if the husband decides to become more active in carrying out household chores, he can affirm himself when he does so, and for being the kind of partner he wants to be. In so doing he becomes less dependent on his partner for appreciation and reinforcement to maintain his changes.

Lack of acknowledgement

The significance of acknowledgement in human relations is greatly amplified when one also considers the effects of its absence. There are different forms that this absence may take. A major one, of course, is silence. Another is denial. A third is distortion, as in sarcasm.

Often we know things that we do not acknowledge. We frequently overlook important contributions or events and take things for granted. We sometimes outrightly refuse to admit what we know. We hold back, do not express it, ignore it, shift our attention elsewhere, lie about it, or even deceive ourselves about it. The consequences of a failure to adequately acknowledge differ in various situations and with each type of acknowledgement. Sometimes these consequences are devastating.

A strong but unfulfilled desire for *existential acknowledgement* can be extremely painful for those who go unrecognized. The absence of acknowledgement that one exists and merits recognition in the experience of another can be experienced as an assault on one's very being. When you behave as though I do not exist, it is as if I do not exist at all. We need intermittent acknowledgement to survive. By failing to acknowledge my existence, you diminish me. It is even worse when you actually deny that I exist. In such circumstances, I am likely to experience you as annihilating me psychologically. The resultant pain, suffering and frustration may be transformed into aggression towards those who seem wilfully to withhold or deny acknowledgement. Unfortunately such deprivation-based aggression only begets more pain and suffering and does not begin to resolve the underlying existential issues. For example, the mutual denials between Israel and Palestine of their respective entitlements to exist as peoples and as nation states continue to fuel the conflict in the Middle East and actively block efforts towards a settlement and possible reconciliation.

The absence of existential acknowledgement operates similarly at the interpersonal level. A tearful man in therapy recently described his experience of intense emotional suffering when his children repeatedly failed to acknowledge his presence in the household. They ignored him when he greeted them in the morning and when he arrived home from work. He experienced his existence as a father diminished through his unfulfilled desire for acknowledgement as a provider, a parent and even as a person. Unfortunately, his efforts to vindicate himself through angry outbursts of resentful criticism simply served to strengthen the children's avoidance and ignoring. Though these children ignored their father, it could not have been true that they did not know of his existence. (In fact, one can only ignore those things that one has noticed and does know about.) Of course they knew he was there, but they chose not to express that knowledge in any form of acknowledgement. Such a failure to acknowledge is, in effect, acting as though the father does not exist at all. This is a marked show of disrespect and amounts to a profound insult. Extreme loneliness and isolation may arise through deficits in existential acknowledgement; this form of non-acknowledgement undoubtedly contributes to anomic suicide.

The absence of *affirming acknowledgement* is usually less devastating. But it too can be painful, especially when one expects and longs for some valid-ation or appreciation for one's efforts. A person's life can become empty and miserable when there is little affirmation of their efforts and accomplish-ments. Others might fail to recognize or refuse to acknowledge one's talents and contributions, and not give the recognition to which one is entitled. One begins to feel deprived, then unworthy and eventually 'bad' as a person – as though one has done wrong because one has done nothing right. This self-deprecating attitude may develop when the failure of others to say anything about what they have witnessed is interpreted as implied criticism or blame (i.e. it must have been 'too bad' for them to even comment on). In time, a person stops giving affirming acknowledgement to themselves, stops recog-nizing their own talents and achievements, and risks becoming pervasively discouraged and depressed as a result.

Certain distortions in affirming acknowledgement can actively undermine one's well-being. Sarcasm is an example of acknowledgement twisted into a pain-inducing distortion. Recently a woman recounted in therapy how she was deeply hurt and withdrew into cold silence when she reminded her hus-band while he was driving that she would feel safer if he used his signal light (when turning left in heavy traffic) and he reacted wryly by acknowledging her 'driver's education lesson'. She had previously been in a serious car acci-dent and was understandably anxious in any vehicle. Having been abused as a child, she was also highly vulnerable to disqualification. On this particular occasion it took her several days to recover. Upon reflection in therapy, the husband was readily able to recognize how he could have offered a simple 'thank you' for her reminder, which would have averted a prolonged period of discomfort for both of them.

The absence of *aversive acknowledgement* almost always aggravates the suffering of victims of wrongdoing. From the point of view of a harmed person, acknowledgement of the injustice is enormously important. The wrongs done, the suffering imposed and the perpetrator who committed these wrongs are likely to occupy a prominent place in the wronged person's mind.

If the offender does not acknowledge the injury, let alone apologize, the psychological costs to the victim are almost certain to increase. A person's sense of worth is diminished by both the injury and the injustice. The victim may experience a jeopardized sense of reality when wrongs, so profoundly important in the life of the victim, are treated by others as though they were insignificant or had not happened at all. Thus the failure to acknowledge is often said to inflict a second 'wound of silence'. People harmed by wrongs committed by others – whether in a family, social, or political context – may suffer heavily and often their suffering is aggravated and prolonged when acknowledgement is not forthcoming.

Active denial of any wrongdoing is likely to be even more harmful. A person who has wronged another but denies that they have done any such thing conveys the message that they might very well do such a wrong again; what they did is, to them, 'nothing at all'. If the victim was already fearful and anxious because of the initial injury, denial will exacerbate these states. There are of course many examples of denial and many forms that denials can take. A continuum of statements that reflects different forms of denial includes: 'It never happened', 'Well, perhaps it happened but I didn't do it', 'It happened and well, perhaps, I was involved, but I couldn't help it and it wasn't my fault', and 'It happened and I did it but it wasn't wrong – under the circumstances, it was entirely justified'. Regardless of the form, such denial is extremely toxic for the victim. The psychological costs of both the injury and the denial (such as anger, resentment, bitterness, a sense of grievance, etc.) are likely to increase and become a focus of concern to the one who has been harmed. The unfair experiences and costs can become a significant part of one's identity and profoundly affect one's well-being.

Self-deception is an example of a lack of intrapersonal acknowledgement. For instance, a person may be informed by a therapist, whom he believes is competent, that he has a serious behaviour problem; given this fact, we can say he knows that he has this problem. And yet he may not admit to himself or to others that he has such a problem. He may deny it – which is to say, he does not acknowledge it. He knows something that is unpleasant and unwelcome. He has knowledge that he is not willing to articulate and attend to, knowledge that he does not *acknowledge*. If he did acknowledge the problem to himself but was not willing to admit it to anyone else, we would consider him secretive.

Challenges in granting acknowledgement

Given the wide range of beneficial effects of acknowledging, and the harmful effects of a lack of acknowledgement, there are good reasons to encourage acts of acknowledgement in human relations. The recipients of acknowledgement clearly stand to benefit – psychologically, emotionally, socially and politically. The broader society in which these persons live may be expected to benefit too, insofar as the acknowledgement stands as an articulation of basic norms of respectful human interaction. However, if one party is going to receive acknowledgement, some other party will obviously have to grant it. What are the effects on the granting parties? What do they stand to gain in the transaction? What are the costs?

As noted earlier, offering *existential acknowledgement* implies recognition and acceptance of the other person as legitimate in relation to the self, or another group as legitimate in relation to one's own group. This obligates an individual or group to take the other seriously. What follows ethically is an expectation that one will attend to the needs of the other. Otherwise, one could question the authenticity of the acknowledgement and the integrity of the person extending it. If resources are very limited and there is a hesitance to share one's resources, one might become quite reticent to extend existential acknowledgement.

Affirming acknowledgement is generally much easier to grant. People often feel good about themselves when they can be generous in their words and give appreciation and compliments to others. A major exception to this occurs in contexts of competition. If I compare myself to others competitively, I lose ground when I offer admiration to them (unless I do so sarcastically).

Aversive acknowledgement is the most difficult of all; nevertheless, it is highly important for reconciliation. Indeed, in contexts where people call for political reconciliation in the aftermath of violence or human rights violations, acknowledgement is fundamental to the whole process. But in admitting that they were wrong, perpetrators may feel humiliated and demeaned. An offender may feel as though they are *giving something up* – the sense of being a good person, one who was 'in the right', associated with a 'good cause' and so on. They may be afraid to allow themselves to be *vulnerable* by relinquishing any notion of being morally justified in their actions. Often, a perpetrator will fear financial or other costs stemming from acknowledgement. Such fears are sometimes realistic, insofar as a person who admits having acted wrongly is left open to lawsuits. (Lawyers often advise clients not to apologize because in so doing they will acknowledge responsibility and expose themselves to litigation.) Thus perpetrators may be reluctant to grant acknowledgement even when they can anticipate some relief of guilt and possible reconciliation as a result.

In the aftermath of political conflicts, where people were fighting for what they regarded as a just cause (using methods they deemed justified in the pursuit of that cause), it is especially difficult for them to acknowledge wrongdoing. They did not set out to 'commit wrongs' but rather to do something else, e.g. 'defend a cherished value', 'defend their community', 'end corruption' or 'free their people'. To admit that actions undertaken during the struggle were actually wrong would be to undermine a sense of meaning and identity tied to the struggle. It may feel as though giving victims the acknowledgement they are calling for is yielding them moral victory. Even in non-political cases, a person's aggression toward others may be something regarded by the offender as necessary and justifiable (e.g. as a reaction to insult and humiliation), in ways tied to meaning and identity. Resistance to aversive acknowledgement is a profound barrier to reconciliation between those who have been divided by injustice and conflict.

When those who have committed wrongs adamantly refuse to acknowledge them, third parties may play a helpful role by offering acknowledgement 'by proxy'. Family members and close friends regularly offer acknowledgement as third parties when providing empathic support. In political contexts, third parties may be officials of truth commissions, boards of inquiry, courts, or persons in non-governmental organizations involved with post-conflict reconciliation processes. In therapeutic contexts, the most obvious third party is the therapist. Indeed, one of the most therapeutic effects in our activity as therapists is to implicitly convey the kinds of acknowledgements that are missing in the lives of our clients. Granted, these effects are weaker than when the acknowledgement comes directly from the other party and hence the advantage of conjoint work, as in family therapy.

Concluding comment

We regard acknowledgement as an important intersubjective and social constructionist process that deserves much more study and exploration. For instance, there is a significant gap in benefits between the person offering the acknowledgement and the person receiving it, especially in the case of aversive acknowledgement. Narrowing this gap is a major challenge, especially when one is trying to enable reconciliation between parties separated by wrongdoing. It is possible to reconcile without such acknowledgment, but that takes much longer and is less liable to be stable. We believe that understanding the challenges of respectful acknowledging is a matter of enormous importance, whether one is concerned with reconciliation in intrapersonal, interpersonal or political relationships.

References

Govier, T. (2002) *Forgiveness and Revenge*. London: Routledge.

Tomm, K. (2002) Enabling forgiveness and reconciliation in family therapy, *The International Journal of Narrative Therapy and Community Work*, 1: 65–9.

Chapter 12

Moving on: forgiveness, vengeance and reconciliation

Elsa Jones

There are three conditions which often look alike yet differ completely,
flourish in the same hedgerow . . . This is the use of memory: for liberation.
(Eliot 1942: 12)[1]

Introduction

For many survivors of childhood abuse a particular dilemma is likely to arise
towards the end of the therapeutic or healing period, namely how to position
themselves in relation to those who abused them and, concomitantly, how
to move on. Moving on, in this sense, entails no longer being confined by
a survivor identity, but being free to construct a life that has meaning
beyond the past and its overwhelming definition of self as someone who is
circumscribed by the experience of abuse.

At this point the dilemma may well present itself in the question of whether
to offer forgiveness, to seek justice, to exact revenge or to work towards reconciliation. Each of these options is saturated with cultural meaning, and I shall
discuss these as my clients have presented them to me, and in the light of the
cultural discourse that surrounds my clinical work in Britain. This discourse
functions in the context of a westernized, predominantly Christianized ethos
which incorporates prescriptions of forgiveness or vengeance which are culturally value-laden. The idea of reconciliation, while in some ways universal,
has recently caught the imagination of the world through the proceedings of
the South African Truth and Reconciliation Commission and the redemptive
yet pragmatic view of human nature it exemplified.

Forgiveness

Many therapists, including other contributors in this collection, have written
eloquently about forgiveness and its role in the healing process. While I do not
disagree that forgiveness may be a worthwhile path for client and therapist to
explore, I will here pay more attention to its problematic aspects. The idea

that forgiveness is a virtue, and is the path to healing, is likely to influence abuse survivors, often in the form of direct advice from religious advisers, therapists, or from others in the general community, who may urge the survivor to forgive – and the perpetrator of abuse to seek forgiveness. This value is embodied in phrases such as 'it is better to turn the other cheek', 'to err is human, to forgive divine', and so on. An ability to forgive someone who has harmed one may well indicate that a survivor has truly transcended her experience of victimization, but for many clients the injunction to forgive can be experienced as a form of coercion.

A woman in her late teens was raped by her father, while living in her parents' house. She immediately told her mother, who believed her, but begged her not to report the rape to the police. For the next few weeks she remained in her parental home, while keeping the secret from her younger siblings, going to work and participating in 'normal' family life. Each evening after she had retired to bed her parents would come into her bedroom, where her father and mother would kneel by the side of the bed, weeping and expressing remorse for her father's action. The young woman eventually became able to voice her own sense of being intruded upon and coerced, her disbelief in the authenticity of her father's repentance, and her increasing sense that these actions were driven by a desire on the part of both her parents to avoid trouble for the father, rather than an understanding of how serious the transgression had been. At this point she left home and reported her father to the police. It was only after he had served his subsequent prison sentence, and she and her mother and sisters had done some major heart-searching about all their relationships, that the issue of repentance and reparation could be addressed again.

The belief that a survivor cannot be free of the effects of the abuse he[2] has suffered unless and until he forgives his abuser rests on the unspoken assumption that the abuser will acknowledge responsibility, and therefore effectively places the control of the survivor's healing in the hands of the perpetrator of abuse. If forgiveness is to be given without admission of guilt or repentance, it asks the survivor to display a truly superhuman capacity for understanding.

Forgiveness can then become problematic for survivors in that the urge towards it becomes coercive, or the process acts to disempower the survivor in relation to the abuser, and also because it may have the effect of disallowing the survivor's enduring anger and determination not to forgive. Thus the decision to forgive can only be made by survivors themselves, and it is more likely to be helpful to clients if therapists keep a sceptical open mind about all the positions survivors may choose to take up in relation to abusers. While continuing unresolved rage may also tie a survivor to their abuser, the option of whether to remain angry, to move into indifference or to forgive and even understand must be the choice of the survivor alone.

Vengeance

While the virtuousness of forgiveness may often be highlighted, there is also a strong tradition that says that 'vengeance is sweet', 'revenge is a dish best eaten cold' and that urges injured parties to exact 'an eye for an eye, and a tooth for a tooth'. Like the desire to forgive, which may tie a survivor to the whim of the abuser, so the longing for vengeance and the desire for justice can also constitute a handicap that prevents a survivor from moving on.

Nevertheless, this is an area that a therapist ought to make available for exploration. Clients may keep silent about their vengeful fantasies, fearing that the therapist (and others) would judge them as unworthy of compassion if they were to reveal their nastier thoughts. And yet having a safe space in which to explore the wider reaches of righteous anger can be a valuable component of therapy. Clients sometimes need to be reassured by therapists that the complexity of a relationship with an abuser, which may for example entail positive feelings as well as negative ones, or may be entangled with a survivor's own sense of responsibility or self-blame, can be held by the therapist. In this way the survivor may feel free, for a session, or for a longer period, to explore only the angrier end of the spectrum. Without such a compartmentalizing many survivors find it too difficult to reach a sense of their entitlement not to have been abused, which in my view sits in the bedrock of recovery from abuse.

How can the desire for vengeance and requital be explored safely? There is surely a risk that a survivor, who is being encouraged by a therapist to explore their righteous anger, may decide to act on this and may then confront the abuser(s), if still available, in a way that risks the physical safety of either or both.

Fantasy

An extended fantasy, explored between therapist and client, may afford a satisfactory expression for a survivor's anger, which allows the persecutory presence of the abuser in the background of the survivor's life to be dissolved. It may also be more practical, where the abuser is dead, or cannot be found, or remains dangerous.

At the end of a long period of therapeutic work B had made many changes in her sense of her own worth, her relationships with her family, and her day-to-day life. However, there were occasions on which images of her violent sexual abuse, over many years, at the hands of her stepfather (F) would still intrude on her current situation. She expressed herself very angrily about this in a session, saying that it seemed entirely unfair that it was she who kept being haunted like this, and that it was time for her to get rid of him. This led to a discussion of how she might do this, and after a few bloodthirsty fantasies about meeting him in the street while carrying a long knife, therapist and client agreed that a fantasy route might be safer for the client herself, not just in relation to her abuser but also in relation to the law of the land.

B had throughout her life benefited from a creative imagination, and had used this during her abuse to, in her mind, lock herself into a small black box lined with satin inside her chest, where the 'real B' could hide and not be affected by the actions of her stepfather (see also Jones 1991). Therapists who work with abuse survivors will know that this creative capacity to dissociate is a great advantage to children, and in my experience this is a skill that can be used and enhanced in therapy to the advantage of the client.

Various ideas about how to dispose of F led to the thought that he could be locked into the little box that the real B used to occupy, since B no longer experienced such a split in her sense of self, and therefore did not need the box. On reflection the box seemed very like a coffin. B decided to remove the satin lining, since F did not deserve such a luxurious and tender setting, and to place him in a bare box. She considered dumping him in a quicklime pit, but changed her mind about that, since such burials were for poor people, who had done nothing bad, and therefore should not be made to lie with F. She then said: 'I know, I'll send him down those dark tunnels where I spent all my childhood years.' The coffin containing F was duly tipped into the tunnels, and a very heavy lid sealed over the top. Readers may imagine that client and therapist were vividly imagining this whole process as it was talked through. At the end B, who had been talking hypothetically all the way through, saying 'I would put him in the coffin, I might do such and such . . .', now exclaimed – 'He's gone!' – and so it proved too.

Ritual

At times clients may find it necessary to construct rituals of vengeance and liberation that can be planned in therapy and repeated outside in 'real' life. The sense of humiliation, of destruction of self-respect or belief in one's worthiness to receive love or respect from others may be such a powerful consequence of having lived in abusive relationships that healing and self-liberation cannot take place until vengeance clears the way for forgiveness and reconciliation. As Martine Groen (1998) points out in her examples of ritualized vengeance with reconciling couples where one has battered the other, holding onto a grudge can wreck the chance of reconciliation. On the other hand, the presence of the therapist while this ritual of vengeance is being planned can act as a powerful external witnessing, and can contain the potential for violence to prevent a new escalation leading to repeated acts of retaliation and vendetta. For many abuse survivors the perpetrator will not be participating in the therapeutic work, and may no longer be alive. Nevertheless, for them, too, it may be that self-esteem can only be restored once (vengeful) satisfaction has been obtained. Human beings since time immemorial have used ritual to contain and symbolize dangerous emotion and perilous experience.

> Her mother's death toppled D into a major experience of depression, in the course of which she became able to talk with a therapist, and later with her partner and her sister, about the ongoing violence, intimidation and humiliation she had experienced from her mother throughout her childhood. In therapy she devised a ritual of liberation and rage that involved smashing valuable artefacts significantly associated with her mother. These rituals were carried out with the help of her husband and sister in a place and at times that carried family significance. Her journey to the 'smashing place', and in particular the return from it, were carefully designed to allow each phase of the 'going towards' and the 'coming away from' to be loaded with personal meaning.

Justice

In my experience a belief in justice can at times act as an obstacle to change for abuse survivors. The hope that the outside world will acknowledge one's suffering, and that the guilty will be punished, can leave survivors frozen in time. It is then as if getting on with life, finding happiness and creativity and love might act as messages which negate the seriousness of the abuse (and yet, one of the most powerful sayings is that 'living well is the best revenge').

Unfortunately, given the privacy in which abuse against children often occurs, and the nature of the legal system, it is well known that it can be very difficult to obtain convictions for abuse, and that even where perpetrators are found guilty, the sentences can be startlingly light when compared, for example, with offences against property.

On the other hand, the work of Inger Agger and her colleagues in Denmark (Agger 1992) in relation to the value of testimony in work with torture survivors has been of incalculable help to therapists working with the survivors of childhood abuse. This method is based on findings in Chile, when victims of the coup against Allende's government in the 1970s were given the opportunity to record their testimony in the hope that there might come a time when perpetrators could be brought to justice. It was observed that the act of testifying, for some, had a profound healing effect. In this context, then, being heard, as well as the belief in ultimate justice, allows someone who has suffered to give testimony and then to move on.

E had been sexually abused by her father from as far back as she could remember until she left home to go to university. Her mother's early death had left her and her brother to be brought up by her father on his own, and his public persona was such that he received much praise and support for being a good and self-sacrificing father. Several years later, when E had spent much time in therapy making her own peace with her childhood, had married happily and just given birth to a child, she was summonsed to appear in court to give witness against her father. He had been charged with sexual offences against other small children, and she and her brother were required to give evidence.

She was in the early blissful 'primary maternal preoccupation' stage of mothering, and did not want to rake up a past that she felt she had put behind her. However, she was told that she could be forced to attend court. Her anticipation of giving evidence was made all the harder because she had little faith in her father being given an appropriate sentence. She knew how plausibly he could present himself, and she feared that the entire experience of exposure for herself, her brother and the children involved would be one of re-traumatization and futility.

The therapeutic work at this stage focused on how she could survive the experience with least damage to herself and her loved ones and, in particular, on the search for a description of the minimum satisfaction she could reasonably expect. She eventually concluded that it would satisfy her desire for vengeance to give her testimony in court, knowing that her father would have to sit there and be looked at by all, while she did so. She knew that he could not be forced to listen to what she said – nevertheless, he would have to sit still and behave himself while she told the court, full of witnesses, what he had done. She was right in her expectation that he would receive a negligible sentence, but received even more satisfaction and validation than she had expected from testifying, and 'having her day in court'.

Reconciliation

The Truth and Reconciliation Commission

The work of the Truth and Reconciliation Commission (TRC) in South Africa has excited worldwide interest and also controversy, emulation and disbelief. Other societies have also sought ways out of past conflict that do not simply lead to more conflict and vendetta. I will discuss some aspects of the TRC procedures because I think they illuminate core elements of what might be meant by reconciliation (including forgiveness and healing) that can be generalized to other contexts. In discussing the work of the TRC I speak as a South African-born expatriate with a modest history as a political dissident, who did not participate in the proceedings, but followed them from a distance with much interest. In discussing these with South Africans and non-South Africans, I became aware that some of the factors that made it likely the TRC would succeed in its work probably resided in some particular aspects of the cultures and contexts surrounding it.

The aims of the TRC, broadly stated, 'were to return to victims their civil and human rights; to restore the moral order of the society; to seek the truth, record it, and make it known to the public; to create a culture of human rights and respect for the rule of law, and to prevent the shameful events of the past from happening again' (Krog 1998: vii).

The belief that this could be done rested in part on Bishop Tutu's concept of *Ubuntu*, a 'philosophy of humanism, emphasising the link between the individual and the collective' (Krog 1998: 285). This philosophy, and the sweeping aims of the TRC, are of course too large for me to discuss appropriately here; I will attend only to a few small aspects of the context.

Truth

In order to apply for amnesty, perpetrators of abuses had to take the risk of telling what they had done, without knowing whether this would lead to amnesty or to referral for criminal charges. Not telling the whole truth ran the risk of being caught out with a partial confession, which would leave the petitioner worse off than before. Telling the truth might lead to prosecution, but even if amnesty followed it meant exposing one's terrible deeds in front of the community, which might also contain one's victims, or their community. This becomes particularly powerful, in my view, in a community like the South African one, where a relatively small population, white and black, still retains significant remnants of a rural, socially networked past in which family and community constitute threads of connection, so that one is known. Therefore to tell what you have done, or to listen to others telling what you have done, does not occur in an anonymous space, but within the community, which remembers.

Reconciliation

According to Tutu: 'A person is human precisely in being enveloped in the community of other human beings, in being caught up in the bundle of life. To be . . . is to participate' (Krog 1998: 110). The mother of a murdered man says: 'This thing called reconciliation . . . if I am understanding it correctly . . . if it means this perpetrator, this man who has killed Christopher Piet, if it means he becomes human again, this man, so that I, so that all of us, get our humanity back . . . then I agree, then I support it all' (Krog 1998: 109).

The Clywch inquiry

In Welsh, *clywch* means 'listen'. In Wales, in 2001, four young men, former pupils of a well-known and highly admired drama teacher, John Owen (JO), told the police that they had each in turn been abused, over many years, by this teacher. He was charged with a number of offences, and killed himself just before the trial was due to begin. The aftermath caused a painful split in the Welsh-speaking community of the South Wales valley where the school was situated, and indeed throughout Wales. More former pupils came forward to allege abuse from JO, and there was considerable frustration and anger, from those who believed the young people, at the fact that the process had been cut short by his death. The parents of several of the young people, the press and members of the community then asked the recently established Children's Commissioner for Wales (CCW) to set up an inquiry in order to allow the children to place their narratives alongside that of JO. This was not intended to replicate the aborted court case, since he did not have legal powers in that sense. His brief was, in my summary, to examine the statements of the former pupils of JO, to establish whether matters were dealt with satisfactorily when they occurred and whether children and others were able to share their concerns, to identify lessons to be learned and examine current procedures in regard to schoolchildren, children in the performing arts and child protection authorities, in the light of such lessons.

Following the lengthy inquiry a detailed report was published by the Commissioner, including a range of recommendations to the National Assembly for measures designed to improve the safeguarding of children in the light of the lessons learned from the inquiry. As with the work of the TRC, there are many important facets to this event; I will extract those that seem to me to be relevant to the process of reconciliation, and that link to the effects of the South African TRC.

Being heard

While the CCW made it clear in his report that the terms of the inquiry did not require him to form a civil or criminal judgement, nevertheless he stated that 'no one who heard the evidence I have heard in my inquiry could, in good faith, harbour any doubts . . . that Mr Owen sexually abused pupils in his care over a number of years' (CCW 2004: 3). He praised the courage of the young people who had come forward at different times to try to make their voices heard, and this praise was echoed by many others, not least by the Secretary of State for Wales in Parliament. It would be difficult to overestimate the effect of such validation on the men and women who had, for a decade and more, kept silent, or told and been disbelieved.

Community

The hearings were public, and well reported in the media. Those who wished were represented by legal counsel who cross-examined witnesses. A number of former pupils gave evidence, and while their privacy has been protected in the public records of the proceedings, their verbal evidence formed part of the public hearing, often, if they chose, in the presence of their families. The narratives of these former pupils and of the adults (professional and parental) who were entrusted with their care became the common knowledge shared by all the community. This has meant that all those following the inquiry have had the opportunity to form their own judgement of what happened at the time. This has not, of course, created unanimous agreement and regret throughout the community – on the contrary, some acrimonious dissent continues to flourish. But the narratives of all those concerned (even, to some extent, that of JO) are out in the open for all to hear and consider.

Understanding and context

In delivering his judgement and recommendations at the end of these proceedings the CCW spoke about the nature and context of paedophile abuse. In his extensive interviews with the media following the publication of the report he stressed again and again the knowledge we have of how abusers operate, for example through the grooming process of children, parents and colleagues, and the necessity for that knowledge to be shared. These statements, backed by the authority of the inquiry, have been invaluable to those who have been abused and to those who work with them.

Reconciliation?

Testimony work (Agger 1992) has taught us that healing, forgiveness, satisfaction, justice and reconciliation may flow from the experience of being able to place one's trauma in context – in other words, to see what was happening between individuals as being part of what was happening in the wider community. Moreover, it is of great value to individual victims of abuse to find their meaningful place in a community where responsibility is taken, and given, where it belongs.

What links the Clywch inquiry with the TRC is, in my view, the social context. In both situations participants in events are required to testify, in the presence of a close-knit community, to the actions associated with past abuses. Legal consequences do not necessarily follow, but the varying and conflicting versions of events, the justifications and explanations for action or inaction, are available to the community within which victims, perpetrators, collaborators, carers and bystanders continue to live or to be remembered. Thus each narrative is heard, and continues to reverberate in the memory of those who witnessed the telling.

The mother of one of the abused young people said to the press: 'When Owen was arrested we were elated, then he killed himself and robbed us. But you know what? He did us a favour. The report has been more wide-reaching than the court case would have been and it allowed everyone to know who failed our children' (*Western Mail*, Friday 2 July 2004: 3).

A former pupil of JO, reviewing the process of the inquiry and his own struggle to come to terms with events in therapy, finds that he now feels able to look back on his school days with pleasure, remembering the good friends he made, the things he learned, and the good times he had, even though some of them are associated with JO. He feels that he can own his own achievements, talk openly about his history with JO, forgive his parents for not having realized what was happening to him, and move on. He even finds himself wondering what JO's story was – how he came to be what he was: 'I feel pity for him, really – I feel pity for all of us.'

Conclusion

Forgiveness, vengeance, reconciliation: three fruits of the same hedgerow. These three constituents of the route to completion and liberation may, for many survivors, overlap. However, for some there will be a crucial difference depending on which path is taken. The difference is likely to derive from personal history, temperament, culture, context and any other of the multiple facets that contribute to meaning and to the delicate therapeutic challenge of finding out what fits for the client.

It is also important to acknowledge that the therapist's role in the choice of one or other of these ways of working is not a neutral one. As therapists we will have our own preferences that will reflect aspects of our own history and values (e.g. it should be obvious that I lean towards the challenge and openness of the process of reconciliation). As with any other aspect of therapy, it is likely that a therapist will lean her weight more behind one choice than another, and will communicate this through all the subtleties of attention, inflection, support, deflection and so on. It is therefore advisable for the therapist to know where she herself stands in relation to forgiveness, vengeance and reconciliation, so that she will in consequence be less likely to impose this preference on her clients.

Notes

1 I prefer to use full first names for authors in order to make the gender of the author evident. Using initials only risks a cultural historic assumption that the author is male. In addition, signifying the gender of the author can significantly add meaning to a citation.
2 When referring to survivors in general I will use 'she' or 'he' alternately, since the clinical experience on which I draw includes male and female clients. In the case examples gendered language will reflect the gender of the client. I will refer throughout to the therapist as 'she', since I am the therapist referred to.

References

Agger, Inger (1992) *The Blue Room*, London: Zed Books Ltd.
CCW (Children's Commissioner for Wales) (2004) *Clywch: Report of the Examination of the Children's Commissioner for Wales into Allegations of Child Sexual Abuse in a School Setting*. Swansea: CCW.
Eliot, Thomas Stearns (1942) *Little Gidding*. London: Faber & Faber.
Groen, Martine (1998) Wraakrituelen, in Justine Van Lawick and Martine Groen (eds) *Intieme Oorlog: over de kwetsbaarheid van familierelaties*. Amsterdam: Van Gennep.
Jones, Elsa (1991) *Working with Adult Survivors of Child Sexual Abuse*. London: Karnac Books.
Krog, Antjie (1998) *Country of my Skull*. London: Jonathan Cape.

Chapter 13

Forgiveness and the unforgivable: the resurrection of hope in family therapy

Jim Sheehan

> ... forgiveness forgives only the unforgivable ... there is only forgiveness,
> if there is any, where there is the unforgivable.
>
> (Derrida 2002: 32–3)

Introduction

This volume bears witness to the involvement of systemic family therapists in a multiplicity of different contexts where human lives and relationships have been struck by despair following the planned, or unplanned, abusive actions of other human beings. Whether the focus is upon the suffering flowing from the range of abuses emergent in the intimate contexts of family life, the violence done by one community, people or culture to another, or even upon the experience of victims of natural disasters where there seems no one immediately to be held accountable but nature or the deities imagined to be represented therein, we are all part of a growing global consciousness concerning the mistreatment of human beings by other human beings. This consciousness, in turn, stimulates a further questioning about what kind of responses to these contexts are possible, relevant, required or helpful. The past 40 years have seen a variety of responses at different levels to these situations that include national and international courts of justice, truth commissions, tribunals of inquiry and validation processes of one kind or another. Systemic family therapists also contribute something to this arena. But what should their contribution be and how should they move in the space between the suffering of victims and the guilt, acknowledged or not, of others? It is in the context of this reflection that a renewed enquiry into the concept of forgiveness and its therapeutic deployment becomes relevant.

While such an enquiry into forgiveness and its resources has gathered momentum in the systemic family therapy literature over the past 20 years, it is a central proposal of this chapter that a systemic therapy discourse on forgiveness needs to remain in continuous engagement with discourses on forgiveness arising from other disciplinary perspectives, if it is to remain adequate to its contemporary task. The chapter has a second proposition: that an enlarged discourse on forgiveness calls for a resituating of the concept's practical space by bringing it into a reciprocal relationship with that which appears to oppose it – namely, the unforgivable. This concluding chapter, then, will briefly review the state of the forgiveness concept within the systemic family therapy literature before considering how other perspectives on forgiveness – from philosophy, literature and law – can enrich the possibilities for thought, action and being of the systemic family therapist.

Forgiveness in systemic family therapy

Despite some receptivity to the idea in the earlier part of its tradition (Boszormenyi-Nagy and Spark 1984), systemic family therapy has seen a slow and ambivalent development of a discourse on forgiveness within its own theory and practice. Family therapists have partaken in what Enright and North (1998) see as a general neglect of the theme across most academic disciplines in the past century. This neglect has been seen by some (Gorusch 1988; Di Blasio and Proctor 1993; Walrond-Skinner 1998) as flowing from a perception of the concept in the social sciences as overly bound to religion and, therefore, not relevant to the work of secular practitioners. Allied to this neglect has been a genuine scepticism concerning the helpfulness of a therapeutic focus on forgiveness for victims of sexual abuse (Bass and Davis 1994) as well as an awareness of the dangers of either pseudo-forgiveness or premature forgiveness for the continuing well-being of victims of all kinds of abuse (Walrond-Skinner 1998). As a response to this caution, Gordon and Baucom (1998) have proposed a determined secularization of the concept via an enhanced scientific understanding of the process of forgiveness. McCullough *et al.* (2000) document some progress in this arena, yet note that a lack of consensus on the definition of forgiveness applies a significant brake upon its empirical examination. Given the state of scientific study they suggest (p. 310) that 'it is premature to conclude at this point that forgiveness is invariably helpful'. Among the few propositions with research support are:

- that a lack of repentance on the part of an offender discourages forgiveness on the part of a victim just as a repentant act promotes it (Exline and Baumeister 2000); and
- that the elderly are more likely to forgive others than adolescents, young and middle-aged adults (Mullet and Girard 2000).

A particular challenge for family therapists who espouse a systemic kind of understanding comes from the struggle of theorists to take the conceptual definition of forgiveness beyond its location in an almost exclusively psychological perspective (McCullough *et al.* 2000: xiv). Two significant approaches to the theme that characterize this struggle are those of Aponte (1998) and Worthington (1998). While Aponte views the act of forgiveness as an intentional act of the will (p. 41) that transcends questions of equity, mutuality and emotions, Worthington gives primacy to the place of emotions in a forgiveness process that is characterized by empathy, humility and a public act of commitment to forgiveness on the part of the victim.

Two approaches to the forgiveness phenomenon that are somewhat more relational are provided by Gordon and Baucom (1998) and Walrond-Skinner (1998). The former practitioners, although restricted by their focus on betrayals in marriage, propose a stage model of forgiveness allied to a theory of trauma recovery. These stages include absorbing the impact of the betrayal awareness, defining the meaning of the betrayal event and moving on towards the future once more. Like Gordon and Baucom, Walrond-Skinner underscores the processual character of forgiveness and advances a model of 'authentic process forgiveness' (p. 12), which is marked by unconditionality (it is offered to the other regardless of their response) and by self-regard as much as by altruism. Along with Aponte (1998), both these contributions emphasize that forgiveness is not tied to the question of reconciliation between the parties to the damaged relationship.

An interesting contrast to those approaches that identify forgiveness as intentional act is found in the work of Kurtz and Ketcham (1992) and Hill and Mullen (2000). Forgiveness for these writers is seen as a process of discovery (the person discovers themselves as having forgiven) rather than as something accomplished by effort and will. According to Kurtz and Ketcham, determined efforts to forgive only seem to entrench the resentment of the person trying to forgive and inhibit the process. Forgiveness, they conclude, 'is spiritual: it is one of those realities that cannot be "willed", that becomes more impossible the harder one tries to will it. Forgiveness, in fact, becomes possible only when it is replaced by *willingness*; it results less from *effort* than from *openness*' (1992: 216).

(Im)possible forgiveness

If the pursuit of an actively constructed forgiveness has its sceptics in the therapeutic arena, the philosophical counterpart to this reluctance is found in the work of Derrida (2001). Derrida's concern arises from what he has seen in recent years as the political deployment of the figure of forgiveness. The last two decades have seen political leaders make apologies and ask for forgiveness from specific other groups or nations on the world stage in a manner too closely associated with the search for certain political goals or ends. Derrida sees the concept of forgiveness as needing to be rescued from, and withheld from, all attempts to achieve some finality or goal. While not wanting to remove the concept altogether from its applicability to the ongoing traffic of human relationships, he wants to preserve the unordinary character – the spiritual, divine, mysterious character – of genuine forgiveness. To those who say that forgiveness itself died in the death camps of the 1940s, or the genocides of more recent decades, Derrida responds by saying that, para-doxically, it is in the context of forgiveness now seeming to have become impossible that forgiveness itself can and does find a new beginning. This beginning is to point to itself as (im)possible, as the possibility of the impos-sible (Derrida 2001: 37). What Derrida points to is the reciprocal relationship between forgiveness and the unforgivable. It is in the context, perhaps, of so many horrendously harmful acts at every level of human relatedness – acts that evoke their description as unforgivable – that the consciousness of forgiveness is brought forth. Forgiveness, he suggests, 'forgives only the unforgivable' (2001: 32). He quickly adds that 'there is only forgiveness, if there is any, where there is the unforgivable'. It is this reciprocity between forgiveness and the unforgivable in the therapeutic arena that I wish to under-score in this chapter. Forgiveness and the unforgivable form a pair and must be thought of together even if descriptions of their relationship pose significant challenges.

In the light of some perspectives from the therapeutic arena mentioned in the previous section which identified forgiveness with an intentional act of the will, it is interesting to note a contrasting view in Derrida, who suggests that if forgiveness happens – and he emphasizes the 'if' – 'it should exceed the order of presence . . . and happen in the night. The night is its element' (2001: 53). In contrast to the view of forgiveness as the production of a conscious will, there is an invitation here, I think, to consider forgiveness as an other-ness that visits us when consciousness recedes, or takes a break from itself.

Difficult forgiveness

If Derrida's (im)possible forgiveness invites caution concerning its too hasty recognition, and even some degree of suspicion regarding the level of human agency underlying its appearance, forgiveness in the work of Ricoeur (1995, 1999a, 1999b, 2000, 2004) is portrayed as difficult but not impossible. For Ricoeur (1999a) this difficulty arises from five key sources: first, it is rooted in our inability at times to reconcile the past as really past, thus leaving our present open to an ongoing haunting by the past; second, it emerges from the fact that victims, in making acceptable narratives of injuries received, forget certain more positive qualities of the other who has transgressed; third, a too strict demand for justice tends to inhibit forgiveness; fourth, forgiveness in some contexts seems forever deferred due to the fact that memories of histori-cal violence and hatred last a long time; and finally, forgiveness is most seriously challenged by the fact that some injuries are seen as unforgivable.

While sharing something of Derrida's caution in relation to the theme, Ricoeur's perspective offers something additional, which responds to the pragmatic character of a therapeutic dialogue that may wish to keep forgiveness on the horizon. In speaking of 'the track of forgiveness', Ricoeur

(2000: 33) proposes a framework and a trajectory within which forgiveness can be located. Forgiveness appears, he suggests, at the end of a work that commences in the region of memory and continues in the sphere of forgetting. Forgiveness, for Ricoeur, belongs firmly in the triadic structure composed of memory-forgetting-forgiving and we may think of therapeutic dialogue, I believe, as remaining on the path of forgiveness by attending to the 'work' at the heart of this triadic structure. Central to the work of memory are all the intermingled acts of narrating and listening that produce the stories emergent in therapeutic dialogue. Carried along within this dialogue, narrative becomes the vehicle by which the work of memory is brought 'into language' (Ricoeur 2000: 32).

However, it is not sufficient that therapeutic dialogue would assist the emergence of a single narrative remembrance of a wounded past. To stay on the path of forgiveness memory is required to assume a critical focus – which, for Ricoeur, means telling the history of the wounded past from different perspectives, and particularly from the perspective of the other or others who may be perceived as the perpetrator(s) of wounds received. It is this possibility of a multi-perspectival kind of remembrance that keeps dialogue on the path of forgiveness by bringing the past into focus in a new way. A critical use of memory does not change the reality of the past but transforms the meaning of this past through a shifting in what Ricoeur calls its 'moral load' (2000: 33). Within a critical use of memory applied to a wounded or traumatic past there comes about a redistribution of the moral burden weighing upon the shoulders of past actors.

At the same time that story becomes the vehicle for a critical use of memory, it becomes the avenue for a liberating kind of forgetting that accompanies progress along the path of forgiveness (Ricoeur 1999b). This liberating forgetfulness must be distinguished, however, from a kind of forgetting that is an avoidance of remembering a wounded past. This kind of 'good oblivion' (Ricoeur 1999a) attaches itself to the work of memory on one condition: namely, that such a work of narrative remembrance is joined to a work of mourning. Stitched into the work of memory as described above is an encounter with the losses arising from a wounded past – losses of capacities and opportunities, an encounter that leads finally to a recognition of some past injuries as irreparable, as losses for which there is no compensation.

The treading of therapeutic dialogue along the track of forgiveness, however, has something more than mourning for irreparable loss upon it. For Ricoeur (2000: 33) there is something about the exercise of critical memory within dialogue that pushes narrators to imagine themselves as contemporaries of past actors who may include themselves. And, in so doing, it brings them fact to face with the open futures attaching to those same actors in the past. Critical memory, it could be said, encounters the future projects of the past – projects which remain unfinished or which were begun only in thought or imagination and which present themselves for possible fulfilment in the present or the future. In this sense, one of the key meanings embedded in a therapeutic dialogue that moves in the space between forgiveness and the unforgivable is the possibility of *the resurrection of hope* – the hope attaching to the future projects of the past. A central bonus accompanying the recovery of hope for Ricoeur (2000: 31) is the restoration within individuals and groups of the dynamic interplay between their pasts, presents and futures. It is the arrest of this dynamic that family therapists often witness in their clients following a wounded and traumatic past. The following brief description of a long therapeutic dialogue illustrates, I believe, the manner in which the restoration of this dynamic can be accompanied by the resurrection of hope within a narrative remembrance that keeps forgiveness on its horizon.

A 15-year-old girl and her parents were referred for family therapy following the intensification of symptoms relating to her food intake and ongoing angry outbursts in the home. Dialogue with the parents alone revealed a story in which a very minor illness in the father during the girl's first year of life became the occasion for the couple's sexual separation in the context of a marital relationship that was generally faltering and specifically experiencing difficulty in the sexual arena. The girl was drawn ever closer into a tight bond with her mother whose bed she shared at the same time as her two older male siblings evolved a slightly closer bond with their father without their relationship with the mother becoming conflictual. An ongoing level of open parental dispute ensured that the daughter never had any sustained relationship in childhood with her father or any sense of her separate development being recognized and supported by her mother.

A consistent mixture of family therapy (parents and daughter), couple therapy – both with this writer – and individual therapy (mother and daughter) – with other therapists – over three years provided a structure of therapeutic dialogues in which the past and its wounds were remembered from different perspectives. The critical use of memory in the family sessions invited both a greater number of stories about their tragic past as well as a wider lens on the stories they had previously made of this past. As the family dialogue gained momentum, the remembrance of their shared and painful past met up with the significant set of losses over a long period that marked both the couple's relationship and the parent–daughter relationships. Yet the mourning for irretrievably lost opportunities became the gateway for an experience of mutual forgiveness (between the parents at first and later between parents and daughter) based upon a real acceptance of responsibility by each for the deeds and omissions of the past. A developing culture of forgiveness within the family dialogue tuned all three members into those projects from the past that were not forever lost: the project for the couple of experiencing a better couple relationship, and the project for the daughter, by now 18, of having something of an individual relationship with her father. For the couple this meant the resumption of sleeping together after 17 years and approaching their sexual relationship again after the same period. Their very concrete hopes from this past as a young couple for having some holidays together and being able to go off on their bicycles were resurrected and fulfilled in the present. Similarly, the privately held hopes of the daughter for an individual relationship with her father found some fulfilment in the present both in weekly lunch dates they shared in the city as well as through intermittent trips together to the theatre. As these projects began to reach some fulfilment, a variety of other relationships within both the immediate and extended family experienced a similar recovery of past projects.

Forgiveness and the otherness of the other

Literature provides its own counterpart to the theme of difficult forgiveness in the poetry of William Blake (1982). The second half of Blake's life was significantly focused on the challenges that forgiveness presented to human beings in the context of their relationships. Moving away from an earlier joyous celebration of the multitude of idiosyncratic expressions of human individuality, he came to see these expressions as problematic in the social domain and indicative of intractable differences between human beings that required the redress of forgiveness (Moskal 1994). In his unfolding reflections on forgiveness, Blake attempted to integrate into the concept two themes that did not always appear to sit well together: the first, a view of forgiveness as *transaction*, where it takes the form of an intersubjective exchange between two autonomous subjects; the second, a perspective on forgiveness as *identity*, where it presents as 'a psychic fusion of those subjects into what Blake calls "One Man" ' (Moskal 1994: 69). What Blake gradually brought to light was a sense that what must be forgiven in forgiveness was not the actual *offence* of one person against another, but the very *otherness* of that person from the one trying to forgive. Blake remained pessimistic about the possibility of forgiveness in the context of marriage (an exclusively heterosexual event in that era) due to the sexually differentiated context of the male/female relationship. While his bias suggested to him that forgiveness had its best chance in the context of male friendship, he saw possibilities for forgiveness within marriage once a couple turned away from the temporal pleasures of sexual love and towards a spiritual kind of love that was oriented towards eternity. Notwithstanding this pessimism, Blake still makes a contribution to the sensitivities of the family therapist in this arena through his perception of the otherness of the 'offender' as the real challenge for forgiveness, a perception which points towards the character of forgiveness as always, and to some degree, a mutual task.

Retributive justice on the path of forgiveness

Within the complex emotional environment of intimate networks like the family it can be difficult to integrate the question of justice into a discourse on forgiveness when interpersonal transgressions have occurred. Apart from specific parental responses to child and adolescent misdemeanours, responses to interpersonal injuries within the family often lead to a dichotomization between forgiveness and justice with the balance, more often than not, being swung in the direction of forgiveness alone. Although reflecting upon similar dilemmas at larger societal levels, and commenting from a legal perspective, the work of Minow (1998) offers good resources to family therapists.

In trying to make sense of the varied societal and international responses to large-scale human atrocities (e.g. genocide, 'ethnic cleansing'), Minow suggests that most of these responses are animated by the twin goals of justice and truth. Yet she notes that an implicit second pair of goals underlying the first are those of vengeance and forgiveness (p. 10). Both of the second sets of goals, however, can be problematic: vengeance, by virtue of its vulnerability to never being satisfied; and forgiveness, by offering itself too often as a substitute for justice, thereby producing an exemption from punishment. The thrust of Minow's argument is that societies, following atrocities of one kind or another, should explore an expanded range of options *between* vengeance and forgiveness (p. 21). The demands of justice do not have to be sacrificed in the hunger for truth following horrific social events. It is not difficult to see how therapeutic responses to a range of family 'unforgivables' might benefit from a similar perspective. In the pursuit of a middle ground between vengeance and forgiveness, Minow argues that the desirability for a society of the goals of truth, reconciliation and forgiveness should not be allowed to shut down a focus on regulated *retribution* (p. 12).

But how can the retributive idea be made applicable to the transaction of, for example, an adult couple following relational injury? Does not the long time-span over which some offences occur in marriage or other adult relationships make the idea seem quite inapplicable? How can retribution work when the 'crime' is one of neglect by one partner of the other over almost the whole life of the relationship, or one of taking an unfair share of income or leisure time for private enjoyment over the whole course of a marriage? Are not these long-term 'crimes' often the bases for deeply ingrained resentment, and even hatred, in adult relationships that present to therapists as having been 'on the rocks' for years without ever sinking? Some of the challenges and rewards of attempting to apply the retributive idea can be seen in the following vignette of a heterosexual married couple presenting for therapy following the husband's disclosure of an extra-marital affair.

Tom and Mary, both 35 years, consulted me following a year in therapy with another therapist. The first therapy began following Tom's disclosure to Mary of a two-year affair with a woman he had met abroad while on a golfing holiday with some male friends. The affair had started shortly after the birth of their second child and had been brought to an end, apparently, by Tom, who did not like the direction it was taking him. He felt guilty, wanted to re-enter the relationship emotionally, confessed his transgression to Mary, apologized to her, and went into therapy with her at her request. They both felt that they and the therapist had worked very hard to throw light on the context of their relationship in which the affair had developed. Yet the couple were neither sleeping nor eating together and had been able to communicate very little together outside the therapy despite both of them wanting the relationship to resume. They contacted another therapist because they felt the therapeutic process was stuck. Mary felt she wanted and needed to forgive Tom, who had apologized, and felt she would not be able to continue the relationship if she did not forgive him at some point.

I suggested that while the pursuit of a reconciliation based on forgiveness following a sincere apology seemed to be an important pathway for them, I wondered if they had not overlooked the fact that a very serious injury and injustice had been visited on Mary. Something had been taken from her in the process of what happened and I wondered if justice did not require the return, or payment back, of something to her in respect of what was taken. Could they both, I asked, consider leaving forgiveness to look after itself for a while, and put some thought into what might be done to repay Mary in some way for the wrong that had occurred? They returned two weeks later and Tom brought with him a suggestion that he would pay Mary something back for what he had done by looking after their two children for six hours each Saturday (the day he normally played golf), thereby relieving Mary of any childcare responsibilities for the bulk of the day. He proposed that he would do this for one year. Despite being somewhat unsure about the whole idea, Mary felt it was probably worth giving a try and she expressed surprise that Tom had come up with any idea at all. She felt six months was a more realistic time-frame for the payback and she expressed some doubts as to whether it would happen even for three weeks in a row.

They returned six weeks later and the payback had been going well, with Mary using her freedom on Saturday either to stay on in bed or to meet her sister in the city to go shopping while Tom cared for the children out of the house. They reported that they were communicating a good deal more and better and Mary expressed surprise at Tom being so 'faithful' in what he had promised. They had also resumed eating together some of the time in the children's company.

When they returned six weeks further on, the relationship had continued to improve. Mary continued to express surprise that Tom had not just dropped the payback after a while and the fact that he had not was a real sign for her of the sincerity of his apology. They had also begun to discuss the question of fairness in their marriage in a much broader way. She had returned to sleep with Tom but did not feel she could resume a sexual life with him even though part of her wanted this. She felt that she had started to forgive him a little bit more but knew she couldn't do this until she forgave him completely. The payback idea had made her think a lot, she said, about what had been taken from her through the affair. What was really taken, she said, was two years of her life when she thought she was married but was not. This was what was taken and no amount of Tom caring for the children on Saturdays would ever get this back for her. It was gone forever. With this recognition she began to weep at length, a weeping in which she was joined by Tom after some time. As the session closed I wondered how they might give some outward and ongoing expression to this loss in their lives.

When they returned one month later Mary reported that she had suggested to Tom that he build a bird-stand in their back garden. This would be an ongoing reminder, she felt, just between them, of what had happened and what they had lost. Tom had agreed to her request and had put up the stand straight away. When I saw the couple eight weeks later the sexual relationship had been resumed for some time and Mary noticed that she 'somehow' seemed to have forgiven Tom quite fully.

While this clinical story primarily proposes the value of retaining a perspective on retributive justice alongside the theme of forgiveness, it also raises a question concerning the possible function of the bird-stand in the couple's evolving process. Perhaps this ritual construction of the stand functioned as a type of memorial to their loss (Minow 1998: 138) which allowed for the containment together of somewhat competing and different memories of the past without having to negotiate these differences as a prelude to going forward together.

Conclusion

This chapter has underscored the reciprocal relation between forgiveness and the unforgivable in family therapy as part of a process of 'borrowing' from other disciplinary discourses on the theme of forgiveness. From Ricoeur's philosophy (2000, 2004) was borrowed the idea of the track of forgiveness which signified the place where therapeutic dialogue attended to the work implicit in the triadic structure which joins memory, forgetting and forgiving. From Blake (1982) was received a warning concerning the difficulty of forgiveness and an appreciation of that difficulty as relating not, ultimately, to the offence of one person against another, but to the very otherness of each for the other. Finally, Minow (1998) provided the exhortation wherein the call of forgiveness in shattered social fields should not allow therapists to be deaf to the call of justice that might be realized through the medium of a regulated retribution.

References

Aponte, H. (1998) Love, the spiritual wellspring of forgiveness: an example of spirituality in therapy, *Journal of Family Therapy*, 20(1): 33–58.

Bass, E. and Davis, L. (1994) *The Courage to Heal*. New York: Harper Perennial.

Blake, W. (1982) *The Complete Poetry and Prose of William Blake*. Berkeley, CA: University of California Press.

Boszormenyi-Nagy, I. and Spark, G.M. (1984) *Invisible Loyalties: Reciprocity in Intergenerational Family Therapy*. New York: Brunner/Mazel.

Derrida, J. (2001) On forgiveness: a roundtable discussion with Jacques Derrida, in J.D. Caputo, M. Dooley and M.J. Scanlon (eds) *Questioning God*. Bloomington, IN: Indiana University Press.

Derrida, J. (2002) *Cosmopolitanism and Forgiveness*, trans. M. Dooley and M. Hughes. London: Routledge.

Di Blasio, F.A. and Proctor, J.H. (1993) Therapists and the clinical use of forgiveness, *American Journal of Family Therapy*, 21(2): 175–84.

Enright, R.D. and North, J. (1998) Introducing forgiveness, in R.D. Enright and J. North (eds) *Exploring Forgiveness*. Madison, WI: University of Wisconsin Press.

Exline, J.J. and Baumeister, R.F. (2000) Expressing forgiveness and repentance: benefits and barriers, in M.E. McCullough, K.I. Pargament and C.E. Thoresen (eds) *Forgiveness: Theory, Research and Practice*. New York: Guilford.

Gordon, K.C. and Baucom, D.H. (1998) Understanding betrayals in marriage: a synthesized model of forgiveness, *Family Process*, 37(4): 425–9.

Gorusch, R.L. (1988) Psychology of religion, *Annual Review of Psychology*, 39: 201–21.

Hill, E.W. and Mullen, P.M. (2000) Contexts for understanding forgiveness and repentance as discovery: a pastoral care perspective, *Journal of Pastoral Care*, 54(3): 287–96.

Kurtz, E. and Ketcham, K. (1992) T*he Spirituality of Imperfection: Story Telling and the Journey to Wholeness*. Nashville, TN: Abingdon.

McCullough, M.E., Pargament, K.I. and Thoresen, C.E. (2000) *Forgiveness: Theory, Research and Practice*. New York: Beacon

Minow, M. (1998) *Between Vengeance and Forgiveness*. Boston, MA: Beacon Press.

Moskal, J. (1994) *Blake, Ethics and Forgiveness*. Tuscaloosa, AL: University of Alabama Press.

Mullet, E. and Girard, M. (2000) Developmental and cognitive points of view on forgiveness, in M.E. McCullough, K.I. Pargament and C.E. Thoresen (eds) *Forgiveness: Theory, Research and Practice*. New York: Guilford.

Ricoeur, P. (1995) Reflections on a new ethos for Europe, trans. E. Brennan, *Philosophy and Social Criticism*, 21(1): 3–13.

Ricoeur, P. (1999a) Forgetting and the difficulty of forgiving, paper presented at *The International Symposium on Memory, Narrativity, Self and the Challenge to Think God*, Dublin, March.

Ricoeur, P. (1999b) Memory and forgetting, in R. Kearney and M. Dooley (eds) *Questioning Ethics: Contemporary Debates in Philosophy*. London: Routledge.

Ricoeur, P. (2000) Can forgiveness heal?, in H.J. Opdebeeck (ed.) *The Foundation and Application of Moral Philosophy: Ricoeur's Ethical Order*. Louvain: Peeters.

Ricoeur, P. (2004) *Memory, History, Forgetting*, trans. K. Blamey and D. Pellauer. Chicago: University of Chicago Press.

Walrond-Skinner, S. (1998) The function and role of forgiveness in working with couples and families, *Journal of Family Therapy*, 20(1): 3–19.

Worthington, E.L. (1998) An empathy-humility-committed model of forgiveness applied within family dyads, *Journal of Family Therapy*, 20(1): 59–76.

Index